THE MAGIC OF
SHETLAND LACE
KNITTING

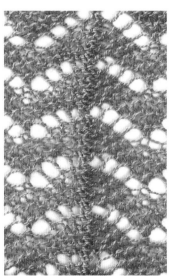

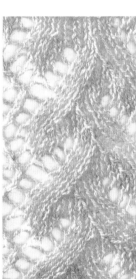

THE MAGIC OF SHETLAND LACE KNITTING

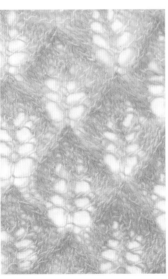

Elizabeth Lovick

St. Martin's Griffin
New York

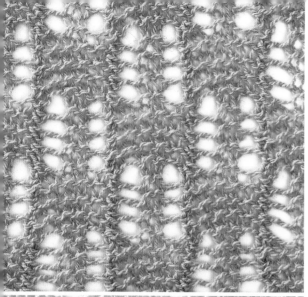

Library of Congress Cataloging-in-Publication Data
Available Upon Request

ISBN: 978-1-250-03908-8

First U.S. Edition: September 2013

10 9 8 7 6 5 4 3 2 1

Conceived, designed, and produced by
Quarto Publishing plc
The Old Brewery
6 Blundell Street
London N7 9BH

QUAR: SLMO

Project editor: Victoria Lyle
Art editor and designer: Jackie Palmer
Pattern checker: Ashley Knowlton
Copy editor: Sarah Hoggett
Proofreader: Diana Craig
Indexer: Helen Snaith
Illustrator (charts): Liz Lovick
Illustrator (techniques): Kate Simunek
Photographer (directory and techniques): Philip Wilkins
Photographer (projects): Simon Pask
Picture researcher: Sarah Bell
Art director: Caroline Guest
Creative director: Moira Clinch
Publisher: Paul Carslake

Color separation by Modern Age Repro House Ltd,
Hong Kong
Printed by 1010 Printing International Ltd, China

Contents

About this book   6
Why I love Shetland lace   8

Essential techniques   **12**
Tools and equipment   14
Yarn   16
The basics   18
How to read a chart   23
Edges and seams   24
Picking up stitches   26
Dealing with mistakes   28
Dressing lace   30
Designing Shetland lace   32
Putting motifs together   38

Stitch directory   **46**
Stitch selector   48
Stitch directory   52

Projects   **120**
Cobweb shawl   124
Hat and scarf set   126
Shoulder shawl   129
Baby set   132
Lacy mitts   136
Ten-stitch socks   138
Crescent shawl   140

Index   **142**
Abbreviations   **143**
Symbols   **143**
Credits and resources   **144**

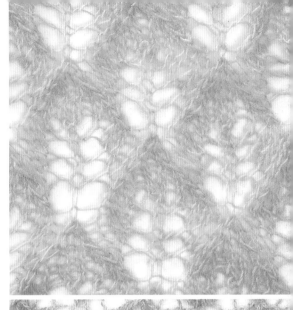
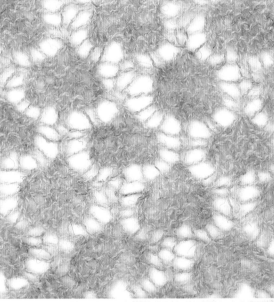
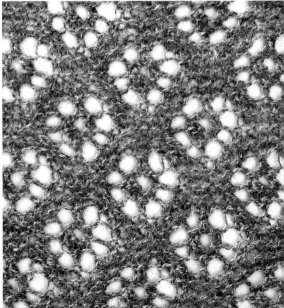

About this book

This book is designed to take the novice knitter from their first "yarn over" step-by-step to complex every-row lace knitting. It presents all the essential skills you will need to master a wealth of traditional Shetland motifs, patterns, and insertions, including Cat's Paw, Candlelight, Horse Shoe, and many more. The stitch directory is organized by stitch and row count and includes a selector, with every stitch shown in miniature, to make selection of an appropriate stitch easy and fun. Also included are suggestions for how to work different stitches into elegant and traditional Shetland lace accessories such as scarves, hats, and shawls.

Essential techniques

This chapter explains all the essential skills you will need to master Shetland lace knitting. Covering everything from casting on, to yarn overs, to dealing with mistakes, it will demystify the techniques involved and give you the confidence to start right away. A section on designing lace will also give you the tools you need to use the stitches in your own designs.

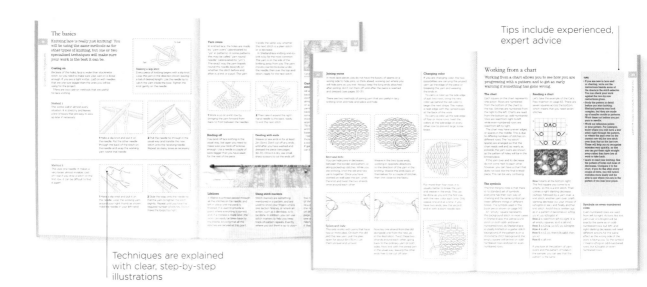

Tips include experienced, expert advice

Techniques are explained with clear, step-by-step illustrations

Stitch selector

The stitch selector shows all the stitches reduced in size and side-by-side, so that you can flick through for inspiration or quickly locate the stitch you want. It is organized into four categories: insertions, motifs, all-overs, and laces, so that if you are looking for a stitch to perform a particular function, you can survey all your options in one place.

Stitches reduced in size

Stitch and row count

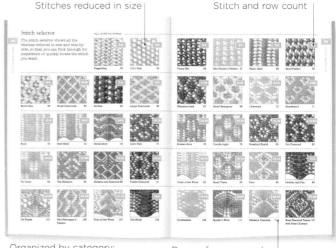

Organized by category: insertion, motif, all-over, lace

Page reference number

Stitch directory

The stitch directory is organized by stitch and row count. The first number is the number of stitches at the start of the pattern repeat, and the second is the number of rows in one repeat. The "+1," or other number, on all-over patterns is the number of extra stitches you need to center the pattern.

A concentration level rather than a skill level is given because, although none of the patterns is any more difficult than the others, some do need more concentration. Concentration levels range from 1 to 3, with 1 being the easiest and 3 the hardest.

Written instructions are given for all level 1 stitches, some level 2 stitches but not for level 3 stitches; this is because, as the number of stitches and complexity of the instructions increases, written instructions become too difficult to read, and the "picture" the chart gives becomes more important.

Charts are provided for every stitch; one repeat is highlighted with a red box. To show the pattern in context, extra repeats are shown, which on the larger charts are not always complete.

Some mix and match swatches are included, showing just some of the ways in which the stitches can be combined. All the stitches are included in the book, so page references are given.

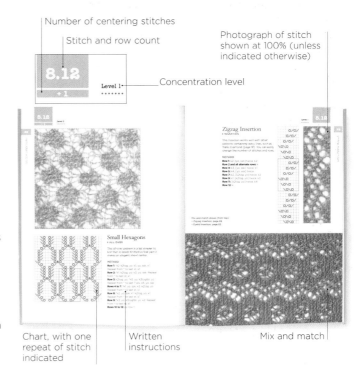

Number of centering stitches

Stitch and row count

Photograph of stitch shown at 100% (unless indicated otherwise)

Concentration level

Chart, with one repeat of stitch indicated

Written instructions

Mix and match

All the stitches in the directory are made using lace weight or 2 ply yarn on size 7 (4.5mm) needles.

Projects

The stitches in this book can be combined and used in a myriad of ways. This chapter presents a selection of stunning designs to inspire you with ideas of how to use the stitches in your own projects.

Suggested alternative stitches are given for each project; these enable you to create unique designs and demonstrate how versatile the stitches are.

Materials, size, and gauge

Written instructions

Photograph of finished item

Alternative stitches

Chart

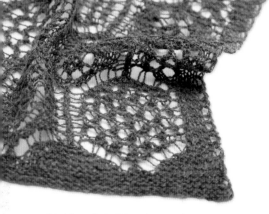

Light and air What characterizes this knitted textile is gossamer-light stitches, finely worked.

The plane is small—only 33 seats—and the cloud is thick. We are descending, being buffeted by the wind. Suddenly the cloud breaks and the bulk of a steep hill seems only just beyond the wing tip. We bank sharply and lose more height; the runway comes into view, jutting out into the sea, the rolling waves breaking in to the tarmac. We land safely.

Why I love Shetland lace

Once the door is open, we disembark into the wind; fortunately it is only a few steps to the terminal building. Welcome to Shetland.

The land is treeless, hard, some would say barren and harsh. Here live a resourceful people, small and sturdy ponies, and sheep with a remarkable fleece. All have been here for many centuries, adapting to the conditions and living off their surroundings.

Fine fleece

Exactly how and when sheep came to Shetland is not known. Travelers in the seventeenth and eighteenth centuries described them as small, with many colors of fleece. They tell of the sheep with "kindly" fleeces, much finer than most, which were very valuable and were kept behind the croft house, out of sight, so that they were less likely to be stolen. Over the years, Spanish merino rams were brought in to try to increase the numbers of these kindly fleeces, but there are roughly the same percentage (about one in ten) in the flock today.

Fine fleece opens the possibility for fine spinning, and from fine yarn you can knit fine lace. No one knows when knitting lace started

Finest yarn In Shetland tradition, yarn from sheep producing the finest wool is used to make the finest shawls.

Heirloom knitting
Shetland lace shawls, such as this christening gown, are gifts that will be treasured for generations.

in Shetland. Unfortunately for us, wool breaks down quite easily, so we have very few early samples of knitting in Shetland or elsewhere in the northern lands. The oldest piece known today is from the early nineteenth century, but that piece is complex, and it is clear that this was no new tradition.

Resourceful women

If you want to get under the skin of Shetland lace, you need to know a bit about the history of the lace and of those who created it. While the folk of centuries ago did not have our technology, they did have our intelligence and ingenuity. Put yourself, then, in the position of a woman in Shetland a couple of centuries ago. You want as much money as possible to buy the things you cannot grow yourself—pots and other metal goods such as knives, for a start. How can you get it?

You have sheep. You can spin and knit. Traders who are willing to buy your knitted goods come through on ships. The better these goods are perceived as being, the more money they will fetch. Color work looks more difficult than one color, so it fetches more. Lace is perceived as being better still—and the finer the lace, the higher the price.

If you lived within walking distance of Lerwick, the main town in Shetland, you could sell your

Lace making A posed photo showing the stages of making lace. The woman on the left is carding the fleece into rolags, the one in the center is spinning the rolags into yarn, and the one on the right is knitting the yarn into a lacy scarf.

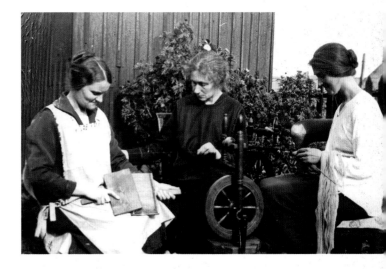

goods to the local shops. But if you were on another island (remember—no ferries), you had to be more resourceful. What could you do that required few materials but would earn a lot of money? The answer was to make your shawls finer and more intricate, so that they would gain a higher price. This is what happened on the island of Unst, north of the Shetland Mainland.

Wedding-ring shawls

Unst shawls are those known as wedding-ring shawls, as a 6ft (2m) square shawl was so fine that it could be slid through a wedding ring. Only a few folk could spin fine enough to create the yarn for these, and only a few folk were skilled enough to knit them.

The softest and finest fibers on any sheep are the neck hairs. These were used for the finest shawls. The original Shetland sheep had fleece that fell out naturally and could be rooed, or plucked, rather than being shorn. Neck wool was kept separate from the rest.

A job for all seasons

The spinners of the very fine wool, like the knitters of the shawls, tended to be the grannies, the disabled, and unmarried older women. Younger women were working on the land and in the kitchen. Grandmothers or maiden aunts would look after the babies and do the spinning and knitting in return for their keep. This ultra-fine yarn was a two-ply yarn, not the one-ply of today, and when spinning you are taking four or five hairs at a time. You have to get just the right

Gossamer effect A fine lace shawl on a dressing frame. The woman behind the shawl can easily be seen through it, showing how light and airy it is.

Popularizing Shetland lace Six young, pretty girls—three spinners and three knitters—were taken to the Great Exhibition in London in 1851 (a series of huge glass pavilions showcasing the best of British work and the latest inventions) to demonstrate and sell Shetland lace, and to the smaller exhibition in Edinburgh in the same year. This popularized fine Shetland shawls in the nineteenth century.

amount of twist: too much and the resulting yarn is too harsh; too little and it falls apart.

The fiber was spun in the grease and usually knitted in the grease—although that depended then, as now, on the knitter's individual preference. The shawls could only be worked on in good light during the main part of the day, while most of the other family members were out in the fields and the house was quiet enough for the concentration required by the intricate patterns. Generally, the yarn was spun in the winter and the knitting done in the summer, when there is daylight for 20 or more hours a day. A shawl like this often took one woman about a year to produce from fleece to finished article.

Shetland lace today

Today, the joys of Shetland lace are available to any knitter, anywhere. We can access very fine yarns made from wool, silk, cashmere, and a multitude of other fibers and blends of fiber. We have the time to knit for pleasure. And we don't just have to use these patterns on large shawls knitted in fine yarn: Shetland lace patterns look wonderful knitted in thick yarn as throws, afghans, and pillows. Almost all of the patterns in this book can be used in this way.

Knitting a wedding-ring shawl is still a feat of perseverance and skill. But with good light in our homes and fingers that stay warm all year round, we can enjoy the process of creation.

Whether you are a lace virgin and have never done a "yarn over" or whether you have been knitting lace for ever, you will be fascinated by the beauty of the Shetland patterns, and surprised at how straightforward they are to knit. And I suspect that, like me, you will never cease to wonder at the transformation that takes place as you wash and dress your work, and see it transform from a nondescript piece into an ethereal cobweb. That really is the magic of Shetland lace!

Wild wonders Shetland consists of over 100 islands, whose rugged natural beauty and constantly changing colors and textures is an inspiration for artists in every media.

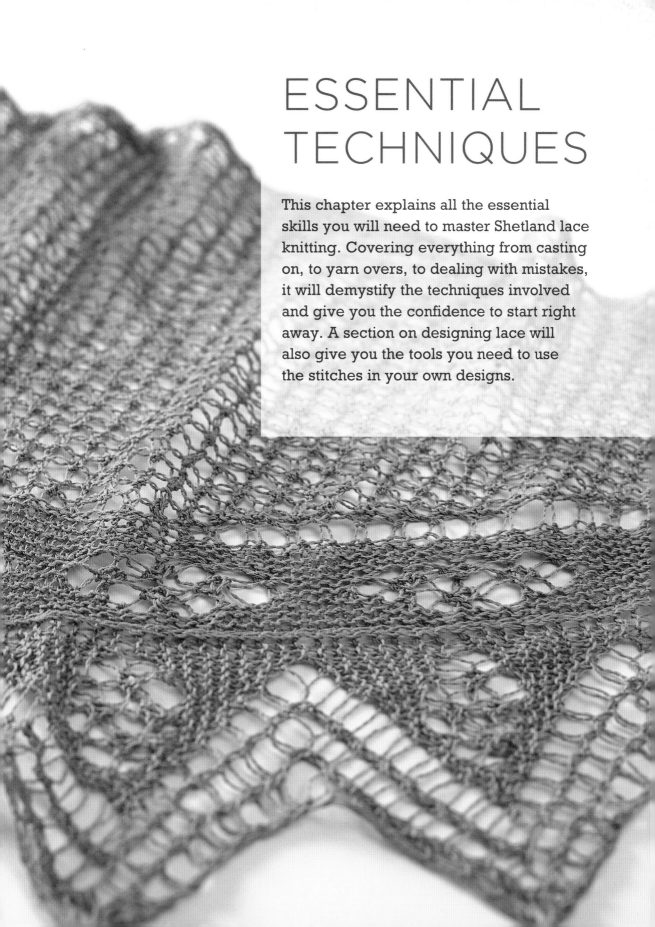

ESSENTIAL TECHNIQUES

This chapter explains all the essential skills you will need to master Shetland lace knitting. Covering everything from casting on, to yarn overs, to dealing with mistakes, it will demystify the techniques involved and give you the confidence to start right away. A section on designing lace will also give you the tools you need to use the stitches in your own designs.

Tools and equipment

You don't need anything special to start knitting lace—you can use the needles you already have. But if you are going to do a lot of lace knitting, you may want to invest in some specialist equipment.

Crochet cotton

Essential equipment

Knitting needles

The best knitting needles for lace are those with a sharp point. This makes it easier to scoop up the stitches for the decreases. The weight of the needle is also important: lightweight needles tend to feel better with thinner yarns.

When you have very large numbers of stitches, circular needles are useful. The brand is not important, but they must have smooth joins between the straight tip and the flexible cable. If they don't, thin yarn will snag.

Stitch markers

Every knitter needs lots of different stitch markers in all sizes! Make sure you use ones that have big enough rings to slip easily from one needle tip to the other, but not too big to be heavy.

There are three types of stitch marker. None is perfect, and all have their uses. The most common type has a ring with a tiny gap in it. This can snag on your yarn, but it is easy to remove if you accidently knit it in with your yarn. Some have a closed metal ring that doesn't snag, but that can't be removed without cutting the yarn if you knit it in. The third type is made from "tiger tail," a thin metal wire covered in plastic. These are often marketed as "snag-proof" but as they are so thin, they are easier to knit in accidently and they can only be removed by cutting the yarn or the "tiger tail."

Dressing/blocking wires

These are lengths of firm, rust-proof wire that are threaded through the holes at the edges of lace when drying to give the piece a good shape (see pages 30–31). They are not essential, but if you are knitting a lot of lace they make life much easier and are a good investment.

Other useful equipment

Odd needles

You will need a selection of blunt tapestry needles in different sizes for sewing seams and for holding stitches when you make mistakes. It is important to use a small enough needle—if you use a thick needle with thin yarns you can pull the stitches out of shape.

Thin cable needles and odd double-pointed needles are also useful for repairing breaks or mistakes. Again these need to be thinner than the needles you are knitting on.

I have a box containing odd thin needles, cable needles, T-pins and tapestry needles by the chair where I knit. When I drop a stitch or break a thread I can immediately trap the exposed loop and save it running any further.

Dressing/blocking mats

If you knit a lot of lace, it is worth investing in dressing mats. These are made from thick foam, into which it is easy to stick pins. They tend to be square and fit together with interlocking edges.

Crochet cotton

This is useful for "lifelines" (see page 19).

Row counter

When using straight needles, a row counter on the end of one needle not only helps you keep track of the number of rows you have worked, but also tells you which is the right-hand needle and therefore whether you are knitting an odd- or even-numbered row. When using circular needles, a hanging row counter marks the start of the round as well as keeping track of the rounds knitted.

Needle size guide

Although not essential, a needle guide is a useful thing to have in your knitting bag. One that has American and European sizes is especially useful.

Large-headed pins

Do not use ordinary dressmaking pins with your knitting, as they can disappear into the knitted fabric. Knitter's pins have blunt ends and large heads so that they don't spilt the yarn and are less likely to get lost in the fabric.

Scissors

A pair of small, sharp scissors is useful. Never use them for paper as this will blunt them and they will snag the yarn.

TIP
- Make sure that your yarn and your needle have a really high contrast. If you have dark yarn, use light needles; if you have light yarn, use dark needles.

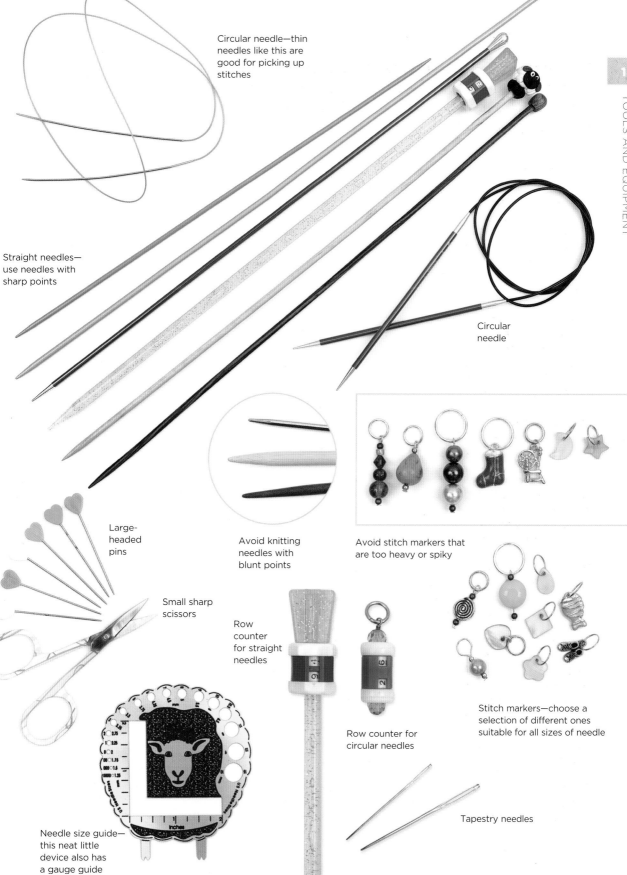

Circular needle—thin needles like this are good for picking up stitches

Straight needles— use needles with sharp points

Circular needle

Large-headed pins

Avoid knitting needles with blunt points

Avoid stitch markers that are too heavy or spiky

Small sharp scissors

Row counter for straight needles

Row counter for circular needles

Stitch markers—choose a selection of different ones suitable for all sizes of needle

Needle size guide— this neat little device also has a gauge guide

Tapestry needles

Yarn

It is possible to knit lace using most yarns—but it might not be sensible! If you are taking a lot of time to make a pretty pattern of holes, you don't want that pattern to be obscured by the yarn.

Wool

Pros: very forgiving, dresses well, drapes well, takes dye well
Cons: not very easy to wash and dry, can be attacked by moths etc, relatively weak
Good for: shawls, heirloom baby stuff, scarves, throws

Acrylic and polyester

Pros: strong fibers, easy care
Cons: low snob value, some can stain easily
Good for: baby clothes, wearing shawls, anything needing a lot of washing

Cotton and linen

Pros: very strong fibers, dyes tend to be colorfast, can be washed at high temperatures
Cons: no drape, no memory, no give, very unforgiving, heavy for its size
Good for: household items, lightweight summer clothes

Alpaca

Pros: very warm, drapes well
Cons: heavy for size, not easy to care for, no memory, can have halo
Good for: wearing shawls, scarves, etc.

Mohair

Pros: very light and warm
Cons: halo can detract from pattern, not easy to care for
Good for: shawls, scarves, lightweight tops

Cashmere

Pros: very light and warm, forgiving, drapes well
Cons: can be difficult to care for, relatively weak
Good for: shawls, scarves, sweaters, etc.

Silk

Pros: strong fibers, takes dye very well
Cons: can be slippery to work with, can be difficult to care for
Good for: household items, shawls

Pros and cons of different fibers

While fine Shetland wool is perfect for knitting fine Shetland lace, other fibers can be used too. In general natural fibers take dressing/blocking best, but man-made fibers can be easier to care for.

Swatch, swatch, swatch

With the many different fibers and yarns available today, all of which have slightly different characteristics, it is vital to try a lace pattern out before you start a big project. Making a swatch gives you a chance to learn the pattern and understand it. It also gives you a chance to see if you will enjoy knitting a large piece using that pattern and that yarn.

Start with the needle size suggested in the table on page 17. Cast on enough stitches for two or three repeats of the pattern, and work through the pattern for at least 4in (10cm). Then bind off, wash, and dress the swatch (see pages 30–31).

Handle the dried, dressed swatch, because it might change size as it relaxes. Tug it, rumple it, leave it, then flatten it out and measure it, especially if the finished piece is going to a lively home.

Look at your swatch critically. Have you used the best-sized needles for that yarn and pattern? Some folk like their lace more dense than others. Work out what you like and stick with it.

Thin yarn, thick needles

When knitting lace, you are making a pattern of holes. These holes need to be big enough to see, and so the needles you use have to be bigger than those you would usually use. For example, if you were knitting a stockinette stitch sweater in worsted yarn, you would usually use about US size 6 (4mm) needles; but for lace you would use US size 10 or 10½ (6 or 7mm) needles.

GAUGE
To begin with you may find that your gauge is very uneven. Don't worry—differences in gauge are not as visible in lacy knitting as they are in stockinette stitch. And as you relax, you will find that you are getting a more even gauge.

"SUPERWASH" FIBERS

Beware of anything labeled superwash! It might be OK, but it might end up like string…. Also be aware that different washing machines are VERY different—and don't necessarily believe the washing instructions on the ball band. At the very least, read the small print carefully: usually, "machine washable" means in a washing machine at 30°C (85°F) on a delicates setting, not in with the normal wash.

BLENDS

In general, a blend of fibers will give you a yarn with the best characteristics of each fiber—so a cashmere/silk blend will be stronger than cashmere and more forgiving than silk.

YARNS AND NEEDLES FOR DIFFERENT PROJECTS

These are suggestions for the possible sizes of needles to try. They are not set in stone: in every case, the needle size will depend on the type of effect you want as well as on the exact yarn and pattern. If you want a light, airy piece, start at the larger end of the range. If you want a more solid piece with definite holes, try the smaller end.

Yarn thickness	Needle size	Use for
Thicker than aran	US sizes 15 to 20 (10–20mm)	Throws, lap blankets, heavy winter scarves
Aran	US sizes 11 to 15 (8–10mm)	Throws, bed spreads, scarves, pillow covers
Worsted/DK	US sizes 10 to 11 (6–8mm)	Baby blankets, pillow covers, scarves, winter shawls
Fingering/4 ply	US sizes 7 to 10 (4.5–6mm)	Winter shawls, scarves, cowls/snoods, baby shawls for everyday use, day sweaters and shrugs, socks, hats and gloves
Light fingering/3 ply	US sizes 2 to 8 (3–5mm)	Baby clothes, socks, shawls etc.
Lace weight/2 ply	US sizes 1 to 7 (2.5–4.5mm)	Summer shawls, scarves, cowls/snoods/mobius, table runners, doilies, table cloths, evening sweaters and shrugs, socks, hats and gloves
Cobweb/1 ply	US sizes 1 to 3 (2.5–3.5mm)	Wedding wear, baby shawls for keeping rather than for wearing, table runners, doilies, table cloths
Thinner than 1 ply	US size 1 (2.5mm) and below	Heirloom projects

Swatches of the same motif, knitted with the same-weight yarn, but different-sized needles.

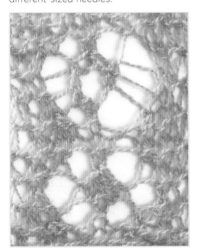

Size 10 (6mm) needles

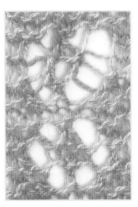

Size 8 (5mm) needles

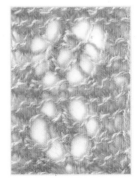

Size 7 (4.5mm) needles

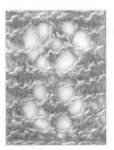

Size 4 (3.5mm) needles

The basics

Knitting lace is really just knitting! You will be using the same methods as for other types of knitting, but one or two specialized techniques will make sure your work is the best it can be.

Casting on

Because of the holes, lace is wider than stockinette stitch, so you need to make sure your cast on is loose enough. If you are a tight knitter, cast on with needles that are one size bigger than the ones you will be using for the project.

There are two cast-on methods that are useful for lace knitting.

Making a slip knot

Every piece of knitting begins with a slip knot. Loop the yarn in the direction shown, leaving a tail of desired length. Use the needle tip to catch the yarn inside the loop. Tighten the knot gently on the needle.

Method 1

This works well in almost every situation. It is stretchy and leaves a line of loops that are easy to pick up later if necessary.

1 Make a slip knot and put it on the needle. Put the other needle through the back of the stitch on the needle and wrap the working yarn round that needle.

2 Pull the needle tip through in the usual way and transfer this new stitch onto the receiving needle. Repeat as many times as necessary.

Method 2

This uses one needle. It makes a very loose, almost invisible, cast on—but if you drop a stitch on the first row, it can be difficult to find it again!

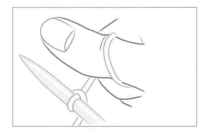

1 Make a slip knot and put it on the needle. Loop the working yarn around your right thumb as shown. Hold the needle in your left hand.

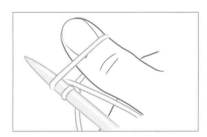

2 Slide the loop onto the needle tip. Pull the yarn to tighten the stitch slightly. Repeat until you have the required number of stitches. Do not make the loops too tight.

Yarn overs

In knitted lace, the holes are made by "yarn overs" (abbreviated to "yo" in patterns). In some patterns this may be called "yarn round needle" (abbreviated to "yrn"). The exact way the yarn travels round the needle depends on whether the stitch before and after is a knit or a purl. The yarn travels the same way whether the next stitch is a plain stitch or a decrease.

In Shetland lace knitting, knit-to-knit is by far the most common. The yarn is on the side of the knitting away from you. The yarn moves counterclockwise under the needle, then over the top and down, ready for the next stitch.

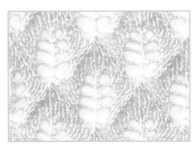

Candle Light looks best on a stockinette stitch background.

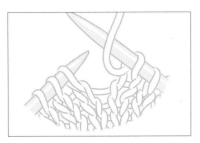

1 Work a yo on a knit row by bringing the yarn forward from back to front between the needles.

2 Then take it around the right-hand needle to the back, ready to knit the next stitch.

Garter-stitch or stockinette-stitch backgrounds?

All knitted lace is "built" on a background of either stockinette stitch or garter stitch. Traditionally, almost all Shetland lace is worked on a garter-stitch background. Fine yarns always need a garter-stitch background. However, there are some occasions where a stockinette-stitch background is appropriate. Candle Light (see page 79) looks best in stockinette stitch, and Old Shale (see page 108) is also based on stockinette stitch.

Heavier yarns—worsted and thicker—usually look better with a stockinette-stitch background. If garter stitch is used, the piece can become very thick and heavy.

Binding off

You bind off lace knitting in the usual way, but again you need to make sure your bind-off is loose enough. Use a needle a couple of sizes bigger than you have used for the rest of the piece.

Dealing with ends

Weave or sew ends in for at least 2in (5cm). Don't cut off any ends until after you have washed and dressed the piece (see pages 30–31). Once it is dry, use small, sharp scissors to cut the ends off.

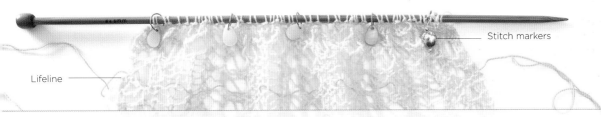

Stitch markers

Lifeline

Lifelines

A lifeline is a thread passed through all the stitches on the needle, and left in place until the piece is finished. It is used to provide a point where everything is correct and, if a mistake is made later, the work can easily be taken back to the lifeline, knowing that all the stitches are secured at this point.

Using stitch markers

Stitch markers are something mentioned in a pattern, and are used to show your fingers where one section finishes, or where an action, such as a decrease, is to be done. In addition, you can use stitch markers to help you keep track of pattern repeats. Exactly where you put them is up to you— too many and they break the flow of the knitting. When you are new to a pattern, especially one where the number of stitches changes on different rows (e.g. Cockleshell page 109), stitch markers every one or two repeats can be very helpful. Use them to help you, and if they don't help, take them off!

Decreases

Every time you do a yarn over, you increase a stitch—so to stop your knitting getting very wide indeed, you need to decrease. In most patterns you decrease one stitch for every yarn over on that row, meaning that the number of stitches on the needle stays the same. But occasionally the yarn overs and decreases are on different rows, so the stitch count varies between rows.

If you want to decrease one stitch, you need to work two stitches into one. If you want to decrease two stitches, you work three stitches into one. By changing the way you decrease, you can get different effects. Some methods give a left-slanting effect and some a right-slanting effect.

In general, the decrease is outside the yarn over as a line of holes moves outward and inside the yo as the line of holes moves inward. Working the decrease in this way gives the biggest hole, and the decreases give the best lines when they are visible.

Two into one

The right-slanting decrease is k2tog—knit two stitches together. There are two important left-slanting decreases—k2togtbl (knit two stitches together through the back of the loops) and ssk (slip, slip, knit these two together). Try both out and do the one you find easiest. With fine yarns you will not see a difference.

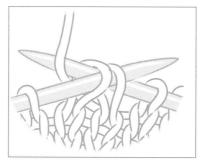

K2togtbl
On a knit row, insert the right-hand needle into the back loops of the next two stitches on the left-hand needle and knit the two stitches together.

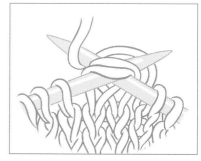

K2tog
On a knit row, insert the right-hand needle, from left to right, into the next two stitches on the left-hand needle and knit the two stitches together.

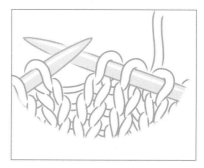

Ssk
1 Slip the first stitch knitwise. Slip the second stitch knitwise. (They must be slipped one at a time.)

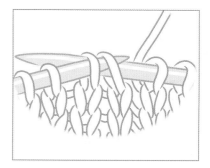

2 Insert the left needle tip through the front loops of both slipped stitches together. Wrap the yarn around the right needle tip in the usual way. Lift the two slipped stitches over the yarn and off the needle, leaving one new stitch on the right needle.

Three into one

There are several ways to do this, but in Shetland lace k3togtbl (knit three together through the back of the loops) is used almost exclusively. It is mechanically easier to get the tip of the needle through the back of the loops, as you are starting at the "outside." K3togtbl is used on both odd- and even-numbered rows.

Technically it is a right-slanting decrease, but in practice it comes to a point.

If needed (such as in Feather and Fan, page 99), you can work four or more stitches together in this way. Cockleshell (page 109) requires you to knit 13 stitches together! When you are using thin yarn, k3togtbl can be used in all situations.

If you are using worsted yarn or heavier, however, you may want to have the stitches coming to a "point." In this case, using s1, k2tog, psso (slip 1, knit two together, pass slipped stitch over) gives a neat arrowhead.

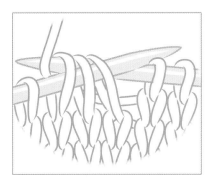

K3togtbl
On a knit row, insert the right-hand needle into the back loops of the next three stitches on the left-hand needle and knit the three stitches together.

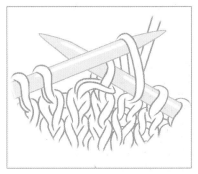

S1, k2tog, psso
Slip the next stitch, then knit the next two stitches together to decrease a stitch. Use the point of the left-hand needle to lift the slipped stitch and pass it over the knit stitch and off the needle to work the second decrease, which slopes to the left on the right side.

Purl decreases

In almost every case, the two-to-one decrease is p2tog (purl two stitches together) and the three-to-one decrease is p3tog (purl three stitches together). With thick yarn you may want to p2togtbl if a right-slanting decrease is needed, but with anything thinner than worsted yarn, p2tog will work.

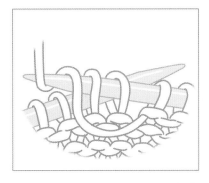

P2tog
On a purl row, insert the right-hand needle into the next two stitches on the left-hand needle and purl the two stitches together.

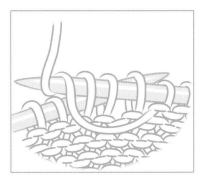

P3tog
On a purl row, insert the right-hand needle into the next three stitches on the left-hand needle and purl the three stitches together.

Joining yarns

In most lace pieces you do not have the luxury of seams or a wrong side to hide joins, so think ahead, working out where you will hide joins as you knit. Always keep the long ends attached after joining; don't cut them off until after the piece is washed and dressed (see pages 30–31).

There are two methods of joining yarn that are useful in lacy knitting: knot and hide and splice and hide.

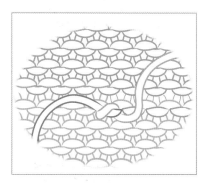

Knot and hide

You can hide joins in decreases, between the border and pattern, or along picked-up stitches. While you are working, knot the old and new yarns together. Once you have worked on well past the join, undo the knot and twist the two strands once around each other.

Weave in the two loose ends, working in opposite directions to the direction of the yarn in the knitting. Weave the ends back on themselves for a couple of stitches, then trim close to the fabric.

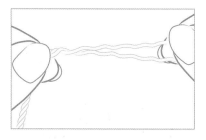

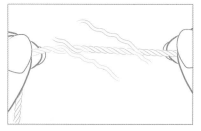

Splice and hide

This only works with yarns that have two or more plies. On both the old and the new yarn, pull the plies apart for about 6in (15cm). Let them unravel and untwist.

Now lay one strand from the old alongside one from the new, as in the illustration. Twist these two strands around each other, going back to the ordinary yarn on both sides. Now knit with the joined yarn in the usual way, leaving the other ends free to be cut off later.

Changing color

If you are changing color, the two possibilities are carrying the unused yarn up the edge of the piece or breaking the yarn and weaving the ends in.

To carry a color up the side edge of just two rows, bring the new color up behind the old color to begin the next stripe. This makes a neat edge with the carried loops at the back of the work.

To carry a color up the side edge of four or more rows, twist the colors at the side edge on every other row to prevent large, loose loops.

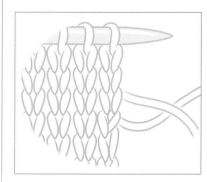

For more than four rows, it is usually better to break the yarn and weave in the ends. This can be done as you knit the first row with the new color each time. Only weave one end at a time; if you have two ends, sew the second end in with a blunt needle later.

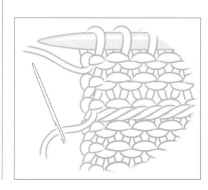

Working from a chart

Working from a chart allows you to see how you are progressing with a pattern and to get an early warning if something has gone wrong.

The chart

Each square on the chart represents one action. Rows are numbered from the bottom of the chart to the top. Stitches are numbered from the right to the left. Charts are read from the bottom up; odd-numbered rows are read from right to left, while even-numbered rows are read from left to right.

The chart may have uneven edges, or spaces in the middle. This is due to differing numbers of stitches on different rows. The "no stitch" spaces are arranged so that the chart reads well and, as nearly as possible, the yarn overs are shown as the pattern of holes will be in the knitted piece.

If the yarn over and its decrease do not come next to each other, however, you can have a chart that does not look like the final knitted piece. This can be very confusing.

The symbols

The first thing to note is that there is no standard set of symbols: everyone has their own way of charting and the same symbol can mean different things in different books. The symbols used in this book are shown on page 143.

An "empty" square represents the background stitch. In most cases in Shetland lace, this will be a knit stitch on both odd- and even-numbered rows, as Shetland lace is usually knitted on a garter-stitch background. If the pattern is on a stockinette-stitch background, the empty square will be knit on odd-numbered rows and purl on even-numbered rows.

Reading a chart

Let's take the example of the Cat's Paw Insertion on page 65. There are seven squares across the bottom, which means that you need seven stitches.

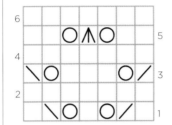

Row 1 starts at the bottom right. The first square you come to is empty, so this is a knit stitch. Then comes a right-slanting decrease (k2tog), followed by a yarn over, a knit stitch, another yarn over, a left-slanting decrease (so your choice of k2togtbl or ssk), and finally another knit stitch. And if this is written out in a pattern it becomes k1, k2tog, yo, k1, yo, k2togtbl, k1.
Row 2 is read from left to right. It is all empty squares, so it is all knit.
Row 3 is k2tog, yo, k3, yo, k2togtbl.
Row 4 is all k.
Row 5 is k2, yo, then k3togtbl, then yo, k2.
Row 6 is all knit.

If you look at the pattern of yarn overs and the pattern of holes in the sample, you can see that the pattern is the same.

Symbols on even-numbered rows

Even-numbered rows are read from left to right. Actions like knit, yarn over or k3togtbl will be exactly the same as on odd-numbered rows, but left- and right-slanting decreases will need different actions for the same effect as the wrong side of the work is facing you. So the symbol / means k2tog on odd-numbered rows, but k2togtbl on even-numbered rows.

Edges and seams

It is often the finishing—the edges and seams—which make or break a piece. As you will be spending a lot of time and effort knitting your piece, it is well worth taking a little bit more time to make it perfect!

Edges

On most lace pieces the edges of your knitting are on show and can form an important part of the design, so it is worth knowing how to make them look really neat.

Method 1: K all

Knit (or purl) the stitch as normal. This method is best when you will be picking up stitches in stockinette stitch. If the edge is to be visible, be aware that every little change in gauge will be seen!

Method 2: Slip 1 purlwise (s1p)

This gives a chain edge. It is very useful if you are going to pick up the stitches of that edge later.

Method 3: Yo, k2togtbl

Put the yarn over the needle as if to purl, then knit the first two stitches together through the back of the loops. This gives a small loop of yarn at the edge and is used in some lace edgings, such as the Traditional Scalloped edge (page 81). It is worth noting that yarn over needle is the same as needle under yarn. So you actually scoop the needle under the yarn as you put it into the first two stitches for the k2togtbl. Only use this edging with garter stitch.

KNIT AND TUG

Knit the first stitch of the new row, then give the yarn a good tug—a really good tug, not a half-hearted one. This tightens both the first stitch of the new row and the last stitch of the old row. If you are afraid that the yarn might break, test its breaking strength on a spare bit of yarn.

Sewing seams

There are times when you have to sew seams. You want a flat finish, and that is much easier to get if the pieces are flat to start with, so work with the piece laid flat on a table.

Use a tapestry needle of the right size for the yarn—thin yarn, thin needle—but make sure that it is blunt, not sharp.

You can use whip stitch or another stitch that gives a flat seam. Look at the size of the knitted stitches in your piece and make your sewn ones the same size. This is usually much bigger and looser than when you are sewing up a sweater.

Wherever possible, join row ends row for row. If you have used a slip 1 purlwise edge, this is straightforward: pick up every chain along the edge, making sure you take the same leg each time. If the row edges are all knit, they will consist of a "knot" followed by a vertical strand. When sewing up, take either the knot each time or the strand.

Whip stitch

With wrong sides facing, insert the needle through both pieces of fabric, taking in single, outside-edge strands only. Bring the needle back to insert through the same side as before and continue. When opened, the seam should lie flat with no ridge.

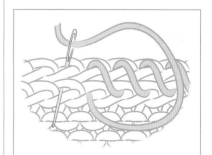

Grafting or Kitchener stitch

Grafting is a way of joining two sets of live stitches which is virtually invisible. Once you know what you are doing, this is straightforward— but again it is always the first couple of stitches that are the problem. Never start any grafting of any type when you have a deadline ahead of you. You might get 30 stitches done in three minutes, or it might take half an hour or more.

Grafting garter stitch

When grafting in garter stitch, make sure that one piece ends with an odd-numbered row, and the second piece ends with an extra, even-numbered row. Prepare by threading a tapestry needle with the yarn and placing each set of stitches on a thinner needle than you have used for knitting. Put the pieces flat, facing each other, placing the piece with the extra row above. The "back" of the stitches is the side on the table, and the "front" is the side you are looking at; "away from you" is putting the needle from the front to back, and "toward you" is putting the needle from the back to the front.

Start by putting the threaded needle down, away from you, through the first stitch on the top needle (from front to back), then down, away from you, through the first stitch on the bottom needle. Now bring the threaded needle up, toward you, through the second stitch on the bottom needle (from back to front) then up, toward you, through the first stitch on the top needle (from back to front); then down through the second stitch on the bottom needle, and down through the second stitch on the bottom needle; then up through the third stitch on the bottom needle, up through the second on the top, down through the third on the top, down through the fourth on the bottom. Continue going down, down, up, up until you come to the end of the row.

START FINISHING BEFORE YOU START KNITTING
Use the spare yarn at the start and finish of your knitting to graft, so make sure you leave enough yarn for the job.

PRACTICE IN ANOTHER COLOR
If you are new to grafting, knit up a couple of pieces in garter stitch to practice with. Graft in a different-colored thread so you can see how it works. Watch the size of your grafted stitches—make them the same size as the knitted stitches.

FREDDY, TEDDY
I was told how to remember the actions for grafting garter stitch by Mary Kay, a great Shetland knitter who taught math for many years. She said that in Shetland dialect, "from you" is pronounced "fray dee" and "to you" is pronounced "tay dee." So garter stitch grafting becomes "Freddy, Teddy!" And how to remember which comes first? F comes before T in the alphabet.

Picking up stitches

If you are picking up stitches around a square (in a shawl or pillow front, for example), you have three types of edges—the live stitches that you have been knitting with, the cast-on edge, and the two side edges. The way you pick up stitches is different for each. Always pick up with a needle considerably smaller than the one you are knitting with. Note that you pick up the line of stitches and then knit the whole row—you do not knit as you go.

Knitting the first row after picking up stitches

You can see from the photos that the stitches that have been picked up are mounted differently. Stitches picked up from a knitted edge and a slip 1 purlwise edge need to be knitted into the back of the stitch on the first row, while those picked up from a yo, k2togtbl edge need to be knitted normally.

Cast-on edge

In most cases, if you need to knit on from a cast-on edge, you will have cast on with waste yarn. Remove the waste yarn stitch by stitch and place the live stitches on the needle. If you haven't used waste yarn, how you pick up depends on how you cast on. If you look at both sides

of your cast on, you will see somewhere a line of slanting loops, one per stitch. Insert your needle across the slant of the loop, making an X with it. This makes it easier to then move the tip back to scoop up the next stitch.

The first and last stitch may have a different structure. This is where you may have to improvise and shove the needle through a knot! Alternatively, you can knit into the front and back of the stitch before.

Yo, k2togtbl edge

Here you have a relatively large loop at the beginning of every other row. If you are using garter stitch, scoop these loops up. Avoid this edging for stockinette stitch!

Stockinette-stitch edge

In stockinette stitch, knots and strands again represent the rows. This time, however, you need to pick up roughly three stitches for every four rows—so as well as the knots, you need to pick up a stitch in every other strand. These can be picked up as you go along OR, better, pick them up and knit them as you knit the picked-up stitches. This latter way is easier, but does require a bit more concentration.

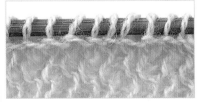

Slip 1 edge

This looks like a chain. For a garter-stitch background, you need to pick up one stitch from each chain. Each loop of the chain has two "legs." If you pick up one leg, you will get a line on the finished piece where the other leg lies. Pick up your "leg" as you did for the cast-on edge—inserting the needle to make an X.

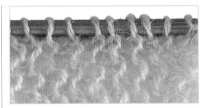

Garter-stitch edge

If you look at the edge of your knitting, you will see a series of "knots" joined by "strands." Each represents a row. In garter stitch, you need to pick up one stitch for every two rows, so you need to pick up every knot by pushing the needle through the knot. It is also possible to pick up the strands instead of the knots. However, it is more difficult to scoop up the lines, and the knots can show as bumps between the picked-up stitches.

Attaching a lace

It is quite possible to bind off stitches and then sew the lace edging neatly in place. However, if you would prefer to bind off at the same time as knitting the lace edging, this is how you do it. It is easiest if the stitches you are binding off are on a circular needle. I am going to call these the "original stitches." You will also need one straight needle of the same size.

1 Begin by casting on the lace edging stitches on the straight needle. These stitches are your "lace stitches."

2 Knit the first row of the lace, then the second row until one stitch of the lace remains. Now knit this remaining lace stitch together with the first original stitch.

3 Continue like this, decreasing one original stitch at the end of each even-numbered lace row by knitting the last stitch of the lace together with the next original stitch.

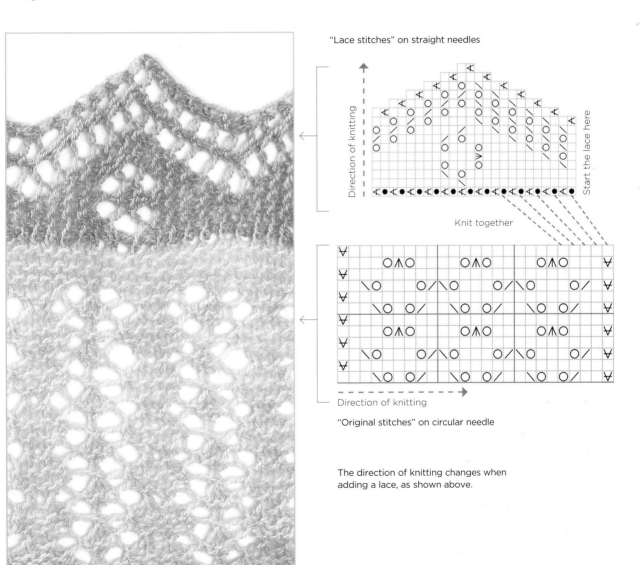

"Lace stitches" on straight needles

Direction of knitting

Start the lace here

Knit together

Direction of knitting

"Original stitches" on circular needle

The direction of knitting changes when adding a lace, as shown above.

Here, the "original stitches" are in turquoise and the "lace stitches" are in blue.

Dealing with mistakes

We all make them! I reckon that for every shawl I finish, I have knitted one and a quarter shawls. The rest is those rows taken back. The key is to know when you can get around the mistakes and when you have to take them back.

Very often, you realize something is wrong because you have the wrong number of stitches. If you have too many, you have probably put in an extra yarn over; if you have too few, you have probably either dropped a stitch or forgotten to put in a yarn over. The key to putting things right is to work out where the error is. If you are using lots of stitch markers, this will be obvious fairly quickly. If not, start at the beginning of the row and count through the pattern until you come to the error.

Dropped stitch

First, stop the stitch from running back any further by securing the dropped stitch on a pin. You can then work the stitch back up to the needle with a crochet hook or cable needle. If more than one stitch has been dropped, or the dropped stitch is involved with decreases, consider taking rows back.

Extra yarn over—one stitch too many

It is easy to put in an extra yarn over, say before a k2tog as well as after. To repair, just drop the yarn over by slipping it off the needle. And even if you have done the return row, you can still drop the extra yarn over with the stitch above. Dressing will remove all traces.

Missed yarn over

This can be corrected on the following row, or on the following right-side row. On the following row, simply pick up the strand where the yarn over should be. On the next row, pick up the second strand down (in the place the yarn over should be), then loop this up round the strand above, as you would for any dropped stitch.

Yarn over on the wrong side of the decrease

You need to drop the k2tog and the yarn over, then "knit" them again the right way round. If you have already worked the even row after the mistake, make the correction on the second strand down, then "knit" the row above with the first strand.

Extra k2tog—one stitch too few

Here, you need to look at your work to see the effect it is having, and where the mistake is. You have two options—you can either take it back, or make another stitch on the row you are on by picking up the strand between two stitches and knitting into the back of it.

In some patterns, a third option is to miss out the k2tog on the next pattern row, or to work 2 together instead of 3 together. Only looking hard at your pattern will tell you what is the best thing to do.

This swatch shows where various mistakes were made and explains if or how they were fixed. However, the important thing to observe is how little they show in the final piece.

• 2 plain rows missed out of the lace—this was left (1).
• yo on wrong side of decrease—this was left (2).
• k2tog, yo worked instead of k2tog, yo, yo, ssk—this was left (3).
• Extra stitch—k3togtbl worked instead of k2togtbl (4).
• k2tog, yo, ssk worked instead of yo, yo—k and p worked in the one yo on the following row (5).

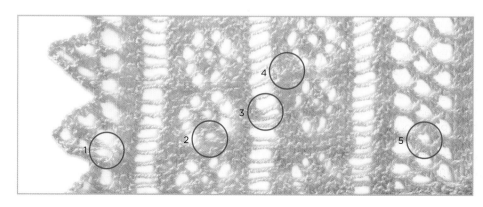

Knit 1 not slip 1 at the start of a row

Here it depends on what is going to happen to the edge. If the mistake is on an edge that will be picked up you do not need to take the knitting back, as you won't notice the mistake once the stitches are picked up. If the mistake is on the outer edge, then there is nothing for it but to leave it or take it back.

Part of the pattern is completely wrong

There is no one right way of dealing with this. You need to take your time and decide whether to take your work back to before the mistake, or whether to just take back a section.

Start by spreading out your work. If you are using white yarn, put a dark-colored cloth or towel under it; if you are using dark yarn, use a light backing. Look at it critically, leave it for a while, and then make your decision.

Taking back a small piece

With a small piece, usually the best thing to do is to take it back.

1 If you have a lifeline (see page 19) in place, you may want to take it back to that point. If you do not, take the needle out and slowly and gradually pull the yarn so that the stitches pull out.

2 When you have pulled back past the mistake to correct work, put the stitches onto a smaller needle than the ones you are knitting with and then knit onto the correct needles.

Taking back a large area

If a large area needs to be taken back, place your work on a contrasting-colored background on a cork board or other surface into which you can stick pins.

Have plenty of pins and thin needles ready. Tapestry needles work well if you are knitting with very small needles, and sock needles or other short, thin, double-pointed needles are useful.

1 Spread the work out and pin it well away from the "working" area. If there are already dropped stitches, stick a pin through each of these to stop them running further. Make sure you know how many stitches you are taking back.

2 Now carefully drop each stitch back to below the mistake, securing them again with a pin. You will end up with lines of yarn above a row of pins.

3 Now use your spare double-pointed needles to knit the section back up, using the strands of yarn for each row, making sure you always use the bottom strand. Pull the work after every re-knit row to even out the gauge. You can leave your work at any time on the needle.

4 Once the stitches are back to the level of the rest of the work, place them on the correct needle and knit on. After a few rows, pull the area in all directions, and you will be surprised how little it shows. Once it is washed and dressed, no one will be able to see it.

Repairing a break

Sometimes you catch your work and the yarn snaps. This is heart-breaking, but don't despair: you will probably be able to mend it invisibly. The best way to deal with this depends on what has happened, what stitches are dropped, and what lengths of yarn you have to work with.

You need to be aware of the use to which the piece will be put. A working baby blanket will need a solution including knots; an evening shawl used occasionally with great care can be repaired more delicately.

1 Whatever you are going to do, first put the dropped stitches on pins, above and below the break, so that, as you pull the yarn to repair one stitch, you will not lose more.

2 You are going to have to use extra yarn to make the repair, so you need to work out how and where you are going to join the yarn. It is often worth pulling back another couple of stitches to get a long enough piece of yarn to attach the new piece to.

3 If the piece is going to get used, either splice along a good 3in (7.5cm) or knot. This knot can be lost between stitches or in a decrease.

4 Now use the new yarn and a tapestry needle to "knit" the missing stitches, and to loop in to the dropped ones. If several stitches have been involved, repair in the same way.

5 Graft the repaired stitches to those above the break. Finish off by weaving in the ends in the usual way and finally remove the lifeline.

Dressing lace

"Dressing" (the term used in Shetland), or blocking, is the process whereby you wet the knitted lace and dry it stretched out. In general, the width of the piece will increase by about a third, and the length by about a tenth.

It is mainly natural fibers that "take dressing well"—in other words, the holes open up and, when dry, stay that way. Manmade fibers tend to revert to the original size after dressing.

A WORD ABOUT BABY SHAWLS

A busy mom has neither the time nor inclination to take this amount of care with a shawl. If you want your shawl to be used, use a good-quality acrylic yarn, which can be thrown into the washing machine and tumble drier. If you give an heirloom shawl, offer to launder it. After all, the original Shetland shawls were sent back to the maker to be washed and dressed…

Washing

1 Fill a bowl with lukewarm water and add a few drops of a good-quality dishwashing liquid to make a good lather. Drop the garment in and swish it about. Squeeze it, but do not wring it. Lift it out and squeeze out as much water as possible.

2 Rinse in a bowl of lukewarm water, and repeat the rinsing. Each time you rinse, make sure that the temperature of the water is the same: sudden changes in temperature cause felting.

3 Now put the garment in a wash bag or pillow case and give it a wool cycle spin in your washing machine. Alternatively, lay the garment on a towel, roll the towel up, and squeeze the roll to remove as much water as possible.

Drying and dressing

You will need a flat surface, larger than your garment, into which you can stick pins. This can be a special cork or foam board, or can be the carpet of the spare room. You will also need quilting pins—the type with a large head—or knitter's pins.

1 Place the garment on the surface, spread it out roughly at first, then start to smooth it to shape from the center. You are aiming to flatten the garment and open up the holes. This means that you are going to be putting the knitting under tension. Don't pull too hard.

2 Once the garment is getting toward the correct shape and size, start pinning.

If the center has holes around it, put in wires here. Remember that you will probably have to take out these initial pins as the shaping continues. This is back-breaking work—don't hurry it!

If you have a peaked edging, pin every single point. Start by pinning every fourth one until all the lace is pinned in this way. Then go around again, pinning the points in between. Don't be too surprised if you find you have to re-pin complete sections.

3 Once the garment is pinned to your satisfaction, leave it until it feels dry—then leave it for another 24 hours before you remove the pins.

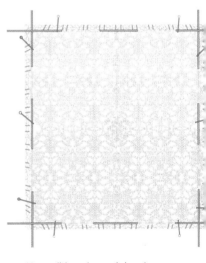

Use quilting pins and dressing wires to give your final piece the best possible shape.

IMPROVISE!

If you don't have a large permanent space to dress your work, here are some alternatives.

- Attach cork tiles to a spare wall to make a dressing board.

- Cover a spare double bed with thick, fluffy towels—the fluffy is important. Start from the center and smooth the garment out over the towels; friction will hold it in place. Then pull out each scallop individually.

- Dress your garment folded. Decide how you are going to fold it—one option is to make use of the lines along the edge of the center and at the miters. If possible, pin the scallops, putting several layers on the same pin if this suits. It will take longer to dry, but take a lot less space.

- Consider pressing. Put a thick towel on your ironing board or on a table. Place the garment on top and cover with a terry dish towel. Put the iron down on the dish towel for a few seconds. Work from the center out, doing one border at a time. Finish with the lace edging, pulling the scallops as you press. (If you are nervous of this, try it out with your swatch first.)

Storing your lace

Once the shawl is totally dry, cut off the yarn ends. Fold the lace gently and place it in a cotton bag (an old pillow case is fine), along with deterrents for your local pests. Alternatively, roll the lace around postal tubes taped together. For a white garment, you may wish to put a layer of acid-free tissue paper around the tubes first, and between the garment layers.

After wear, leave it folded carefully over a chair for 24 hours, then put it back in its bag. If you have dressed the garment well, when it needs washing again you will not need to take the same amount of care; dry it flat, folded if necessary, but you should not need to pin the scallops.

Aftercare

It is a good idea to keep a ball band from each project you complete as a reference for washing instructions, or alternatively make a note of them. Standard laundering symbols are given below, although you may prefer to wash your knitted item by hand. If so, this should be done gently in hot water, with a mild, detergent-free cleaning agent. Most purpose-made wool or fabric shampoos are ideal, but check the one you choose does not contain optical brighteners, which will cause yarn colors to fade. Always rinse the piece thoroughly and allow it to dry naturally.

STANDARD LAUNDERING SYMBOLS

Hand Washing	Machine Washing	Bleaching	Pressing	Dry Cleaning
Do not wash by hand or machine	Machine washable in warm water at the stated temperature	Bleaching not permitted	Do not press	Do not dry clean
Hand washable in warm water at the stated temperature	Machine washable in warm water at the stated temperature, cool rinse and short spin	Bleaching permitted (with chlorine)	Press with a cool iron	May be dry cleaned with all solutions
	Machine washable in warm water at the stated temperature, short spin		Press with a warm iron	May be dry cleaned with perchlorethylene or fluorocarbon- or petroleum-based solvents
			Press with a hot iron	May be dry cleaned with fluorocarbon- or petroleum-based solvents only

Designing Shetland lace

Putting the right patterns together in the right way is the key to good design. A lot of it is trial and error and swatching—no one gets it right all the time. However, there are some guidelines that can help you.

Please note that, for ease, I will use the word "shawl" throughout. The process is exactly the same for a scarf or table runner, doily or throw, baby blanket or wedding veil.

Basics

Regardless of what you want to make, during the design process you will have to pose and answer five questions:

• What shape do I want the piece to be?
• What yarn do I want to use?
• What patterns do I want to use?
• What gauge do I want to use?
• How big do I want the piece to be?

With different projects you will answer these questions in different orders. For example, if you have two skeins of hand-dyed yarn in your stash, everything else has to work around that. On the other hand, if you want a table cloth for your circular table, start with the shape.

In practice, you look at the five questions together—but for ease we will look at them separately.

What shape?

There are three families:
Triangles—narrow, wide, shallow, deep
Squares—which includes rectangles
Circles—which includes semi-circles

Other shapes are a combination of these—for example, ovals, the Faroese shawl shaping, hexagons etc.

What yarn?

Any yarn can be used for a lace project, but some will work better than others. There are two things you need to think about—the thickness and the fiber.

In general, the heavier the wear a piece will get, the heavier the yarn you start with should be. It is possible to knit a throw for the cat's couch out of gossamer thread, but it isn't necessarily sensible.

When it comes to the composition of the yarn, think about the use to which the final item will be put— in particular, how often will it be washed and by whom? You might want to knit a cobweb cashmere or merino baby jacket, but moms rarely have the time or energy to hand-wash and to take care of fine lace. If you are knitting something as a gift, think of the recipient rather than yourself.

What patterns?

The really tricky part of designing lace projects is finding the right stitch patterns to go with the right yarn for the right projects. Not all published designs are good ones. Not all antique designs are good ones, either.

Start with your own skill level. If you have only ever done a six-stitch, six-row pattern repeat with no wrong-side yarn overs, then don't try to do something extremely complex with no pattern repeat and yarn overs every other stitch.

If you are new to designing lace pieces, staying in one tradition can help you combine stitch patterns that work well together. Once you know what you are doing, you can put Estonian with Shetland with American with Spanish and you might be fine.

If in doubt, go for simplicity. If you look at antique shawls or their photos, you will see that the ones that work best are the least fussy. The stitch patterns may be complex, but they are put together in a relatively simple way.

Be critical of your swatches. Once I have knitted up my swatch, I wash and block it, then leave it for a few days, preferably doing other knitting in the meantime. Then I look at the swatch again. I ask myself: Is it as good as I thought it was? If the honest answer is no, then try to work out what is wrong, put it right, then go ahead.

What gauge?

I remember being in on a "discussion" between two Unst knitters, both life-long experts in the field, about whether a piece one of them was knitting was at the right gauge or whether it would have been better on bigger needles. Both had their own view and neither was going to give ground!

Often, there is no right or wrong—just different choices. Only you know what visual effect you are after, and how you like to knit. You do need to take some account of what the piece is for (you need to be able to see through a wedding veil, for example) but, apart from that, it is very much a case of personal choice—although the yarn thickness and weight will also affect your choice.

What size?

How big do you want it to be? How big does it need to be? The final size of the piece will often affect the choice of stitch patterns. A huge stitch repeat often looks wrong on a small piece. There is no point going for a border 5in (13cm) wide when the finished piece will only be 8in (20cm) square.

The following rules hold good in almost all situations. You can break them, but be aware that it is not easy to do so and still end up with a good design.

- **Thick yarn, simpler pattern**
  All-over patterns work well with thick yarns. Keep both the stitch repeat and the row repeat small. In general, about 10 stitches is a good maximum. Old Shale, with an 18-stitch repeat, does work well, but it has only four rows....

- **Fancy yarn, simpler pattern**
  This is true both for yarns with detail (such as mohair, thick-and-thin etc.) and for yarns with color changes. Sock yarn can be used to good effect—but again, keep the stitch patterns simple.

- **Tie in pattern elements**
  To make a piece hold together, try to tie in elements of the stitch patterns between the center, border, and edging of the piece. This might be a motif (for example, Cat's Paw) or a shape (such as diamonds). These elements don't have to be in all three sections, but it is often a good idea to have some connection between the center and the lace especially.

- **Don't have a design that is all holes**
  The best designs have solid areas to balance out the holes! You need to be able to see individual shapes and motifs, and if you don't have enough space between them it can all look very messy: you see only holes, not a pattern of holes.

Construction shapes

I will be using the words the Shetlanders use for parts of a shawl: center for the main bulk of the piece, border for the section around the center, and lace for the outside edging. Not every piece will have all three sections, but it is often useful to think in these terms when designing.

Circles

Almost all circular pieces are worked from the center out.
Here, the decision is whether to make radial or tiered increases.
Whichever way you work your shawl, you have the choice of a lace edging knitted straight down, or one knitted sideways.

Radial increase

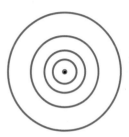

Tiered increase

Radial increases

Here, you divide the piece into different segments and increase at these points regularly throughout the shawl. This means that the stitch numbers increase by a few every few rows.

If you are working with a stockinette-stitch background, you will need to increase six stitches every other round. If you are working with a garter-stitch background, you will need to increase eight or nine stitches every other round. Those are the basic ratios. You can, however, alter them slightly. For example, often you will increase 12 stitches (six panels with two increases) every fourth round on a stockinette-stitch background.

Radial increases work well if you are using several separate motifs, or where you want to create a spoked design. They do not work so well for all-over designs.

Tiered increases

Here, you increase a lot of stitches on a few rows, with large numbers of rows between. You effectively have a block with the same number of stitches, then an increase row, then another block with a set, larger number of stitches.

These give a series of concentric circles. Each ring has a set number of stitches, and continuous designs in that segment work well. The width of the bands can be varied to suit. In each case, the diameter and circumference of the end of the band needs to be known, and the stitch numbers worked to that.

Tiered designs work well for all-over patterns in bands, and have the advantage that changes of stitch numbers happen on specific rows only. This makes both designing and knitting easier. It also allows for shaping—for example, you can achieve a cylinder shape for table cloths or shawls fitted on the shoulders.

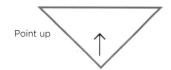

Point up

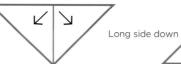

Long side down

Triangles

Knitted triangles can be a variety of shapes, but they are usually variations of isosceles triangles—that is, they have two edges the same length. In addition, triangular shawls are often themselves made up of other triangles. This means that constructions need to be thought out thoroughly.

There are two possibilities—point up and long side (hypotenuse) down. Variations of the point up are usually used (yarn overs increase stitch numbers easily), but this can look like top down.

Point up

Here you start at the tip, and work upward, the longest edge of the triangle being on the needle at any one time. Increases are made on or near each edge.

The rate of increase gives you the shape. With a garter-stitch background, the rate of the usual half square is one stitch per row—more usually, two stitches every other row. If you use this rate of increase for a stockinette-stitch piece, you will get a narrower triangle.

Although the diagram above right looks like hypotenuse down—the shawl is actually made as TWO triangles from the POINT UP.

Long side down

This where you work from the longest side toward the point. It is less flexible than the other way; you need to have the whole piece fully designed before you start.

The decreases are made at the edges of the triangle. This might be at the two edges of the knitting, or the piece can be broken down into two or more sections, giving decreases within the rows.

> **NOT SURE IF YOU HAVE ENOUGH YARN?**
> Use a center-out method for squares and circles, tip up for triangles, and either lengthways or sideways for scarves.

Center square

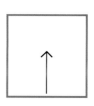

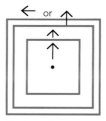

Center out

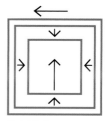

Outside in

Squares

The ways to knit squares are many and various, but they basically fall into two categories: center out and outside in.

Center square

If you have a shawl with center, border, and edging, you can knit the center square in several ways: center out (basically four triangles); corner to corner, increasing then decreasing; straight up from one edge. There are many different variations on these themes.

Center out

This is the traditional method for hap shawls, the working shawls worn by Shetland women every day for centuries (to "hap" means to wrap up for warmth). Here the center is knitted first, then the borders are picked up around the center and worked outward. The four borders may be knitted individually, with the miters sewn later, or they may be knitted together in the round. The edging may also be knitted outward, or may be knitted on sideways.

Outside in

This is the traditional Shetland method for fine shawls. The lace edging is knitted first, either in one piece or in four separate pieces. Stitches are then picked up along the straight edge, and the four border pieces are knitted on.

The center is then knitted from the final border. The live stitches from the completed center are grafted to the opposite border, and the side border stitches are sewn to the sides of the center.

Note that with fine shawls the side stitches traditionally were not knitted off, as this forms too thick a ridge.

Putting motifs together

Once you have the basic ideas of the shape and construction method for your piece, you need to finalize the stitch patterns you will use.

Usually you will find a stitch pattern you MUST use when you flick through the Stitch Directory! When this is the case, start from there, noting the number of stitches and the number of rows in the pattern. Then jot down other stitches you like and which you think may go with it, remembering the "rules" on page 40.

Now you need to do some math. Don't be frightened of the numbers—a calculator and piece of paper is all you need. Start with the biggest pattern and jot down the number of stitches and rows it contains. For a shawl or scarf with a lace each side, look at the number of ROWS first. To make your life easy, choose a lace with the same number of rows, or a number which multiplies up to that number.

For example, say you wanted to use Horse Shoe (page 76) as your center. That has a repeat of 10 sts and 8 rows. If the lace is going to each side, you ideally want a ROW repeat for 4, 8 or 16—for example Wave Lace (page 87) has an 11 st, 16 row repeat, and Cyprus (page 89) has a 12 st, 8 row repeat. If you used Wave Lace, you would work ONE repeat of the Wave lace to TWO repeats of the Horseshoe. If you wanted to use Irish lace (page 113), which has a 20 st, 12 row repeat, then you could work TWO repeats of the lace to THREE repeats of the center.

SWATCHING

You need to swatch for several things: needle size/gauge, look of stitch pattern, placing of stitch patterns, grouping of stitch patterns, interaction between stitch pattern and yarn, and the general look of the whole thing put together. The bigger and more important the piece, the more swatching you need to do.

Once you know roughly what you want, it is worth making a sampler of the stitches you will use in the way you will use them. For a square shawl, for example, this means a piece with a bit of the center attached to a bit of the border attached to a bit of the edging. For a radial shawl, you need to make a pizza segment. These pieces do not have to be full size, but they do have to be big enough for you to see how the final piece will work.

Designing shawls

Designing a whole shawl is just one step further down the line. The center will be either one all-over pattern or a repeating set of motifs. The lace will be something to tie in with the center, so the only tricky bit is the border. Almost all Shetland shawls were square and, as a rule of thumb, the width of the center is about twice the width of the border. Once you have decided on the size of the finished shawl, decide on the center pattern. Make allowances for edges—start, finish, and both side edges—and you will come up with a number of stitches for the shorter edge of the border. Next, work out the number of stitches you want for the longer edge of the border.

At this point—before you have designed the border—decide on the lace and how you are going to cope with the corners. If the lace is narrow—about 1in (2.5cm) wide or less at the narrowest point—you can just keep knitting round the corner as you have done along the edges.

Just make sure you have a complete number of repeats on each side, so that the narrowest point comes on the corner. If you have a wider lace, you will either need to gather the corner or to miter it. Gathering it means that you will need to have some rows where you don't decrease the last stitch of the lace with the next of the border. This effectively gives more fabric to the outer edge of the lace. Now that you have sorted the initial and final numbers of stitches for the border, you can make your design within these parameters. Put in the biggest motifs first, then fill in the gaps, perhaps using some of the same design elements used in the center and lace. This is the tricky bit, and it can make or break the whole design. Trial and error (swatching!) will help here, as will a good eye. Experience helps, but none of these things alone will guarantee success. Remember all that has already been said about design, and give it a try!

Designing Shetland scarves and stoles

Shetland scarves have fancy ends, or tails, with a less complex all-over pattern for the part that goes behind the neck. That bit is not seen, so there is no point in making it complex. Stoles are wider scarves, but their centers are more visible, and they often have a lace edging like a shawl.

Your tails are your palette! Decide on the size and play on paper. Once you think you might be right, knit a swatch. At that point, decide on the central pattern, and knit one tail with the central panel attached. Leave the stitches live, and knit a second tail exactly like the first. Then graft the two sets of live stitches together.

Charting

When you chart your designs, try to get a grid that gives you a good idea of what the final piece will actually look like.

Charting the middle

There are several graph-paper programs available, so make the size of the squares actually correspond with the size of your stitches. If you are working in garter stitch and have no holes on alternate rows, consider charting the right-side rows only using squares: if you are working in stockinette stitch or you have holes on all rows you will need to chart the right-side and the wrong-side rows.

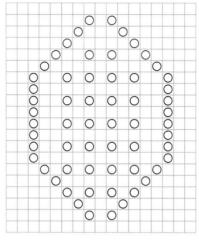

1 Start by charting the holes. That is what the knitted piece is about— holes on a background. Look at the pattern that the yarn over symbols make.

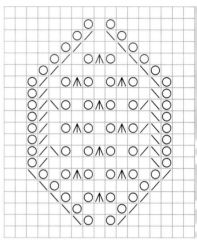

2 Once you add the decreases and so on, your eye sees all the symbols in the chart: it is not the same in the knitted piece.

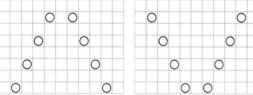 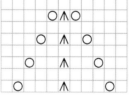 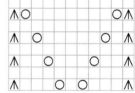

Charting the edges

1 In a shaped piece, work out the main, full patterns first, then look at the edges. For example, let's look at a pattern like Horse Shoe (page 76). The pattern repeat here is 10 stitches and there are two places where it could "start" and "finish"— between the shoes or beginning and end.

2 The decreases cause no problems in the middle of the shoe, where full patterns are used.

3 If we put k3togtbl decreases at the ends of the patterns we will lose two stitches per row.

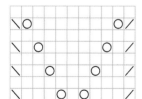

4 Instead, we need single decreases (k2tog and ssk).
 Having to change double decreases to singles is common on the edges of patterns. If you look through the stitch selector you will see such changes time and time again.

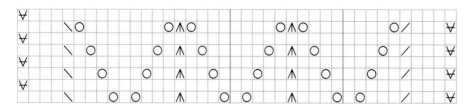

5 To make your chart into that for a scarf, for example, just add a few garter stitches each side.

Charting triangles

Fitting stitch patterns into triangles is more difficult. Trial and error is your only way forward! If you want an easy life, go for patterns that easily fit the shape of the triangle you are making. For example, if you are increasing at each end of alternate rows, using Horse Shoe as above will work well.

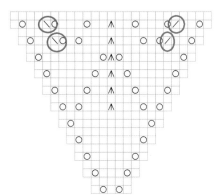

1 As before, start with the holes. The shape of the triangle will be made by having a yarn over without a decrease at each end of every other row. Put these in first, then put in the yarn overs of the stitch pattern you hope to use. Next, add the decreases, making sure you get the "edges" right. Note the single decreases (circled) to keep the stitch count correct.

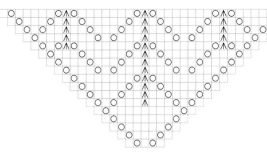

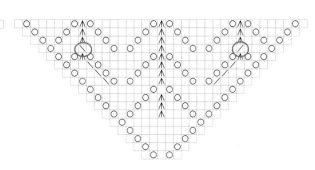

2 If you are working in garter stitch and have holes only on odd-numbered rows, it can be easier to chart only the odd-numbered rows. Make sure you know which type of chart you are using; you cannot use this "shorthand" if you have any holes on even-numbered rows (for example, on the edges of the Crescent Shawl project on pages 140–141).

3 Follow the same procedure as before, putting in all the holes first, then adding the probable decreases. Then check your chart carefully, and adjust the decreases to keep the stitch count correct; here, a couple of single decreases are needed instead of the double decrease.

Making adjustments

If you are using motifs, very often adjusting the spacing between the motifs gives a more pleasing result.

For example, if you are using a bead in a crescent shawl, adjusting the spacing between the beads from one knit stitch to five gives neat edges. Remember that here EVERY row is charted and there are holes on EVERY row.

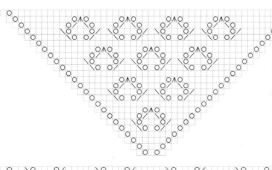

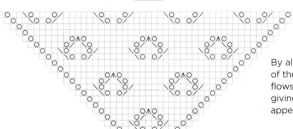

With one knit stitch between the beads, the pattern of holes does not match the pattern of increases and you are left with uneven areas of garter stitch at the edges of the shawl.

By altering the spacing of the beads, the pattern flows over the whole fabric giving a much more appealing look.

Putting motifs together

Once you know the theory, it's time to put it into practice! The stitches in this book can be combined in almost limitless ways. The following pages contain just a few examples. The thought process behind the designs is explained in order to give you the confidence and inspiration to design your own Shetland lace.

Pale blue swatch: Cat's Paw Insertion (page 65), Ladder Insertion (page 53), Cat's Paw Lace (page 72)

Pale green swatch: Cat's Paw Insertion (page 65), Cat's Paw Lace (page 72)

Pale purple swatch: Flee Insertion (page 73), Flee Motif (page 62)

Dark blue swatch: Hexagon Frame (page 97) with Large Diamonds (page 66), Bead Pattern (page 59), Fancy Net (page 56), Spider Insertion (page 73), Lace Hole Insertion (page 66)

Gray swatch: Cat's Paw (page 77), Cat's Paw Insertion (page 65)

Designing with frames

This is a 16 st, 24 row all-over hexagon frame. In the hexagons I have placed various motifs and all-over patterns.

As you can see from the photo, using yo, k3togtbl, yo for the vertical lines of the frames makes the frames stand out. Some patterns, like lace holes and fancy net, fill the hexagon holes while others, like the large diamond, form a shape within the frame. Motifs such as the spider and bead give a stripe of pattern with solid areas each side.

If you look at neighboring frames, you can see that if every frame was filled with fancy net or with lace holes, the effect would be one of plenty of holes but no pattern! If, however, you alternated the two patterns, the effect would be much easier on the eye. Similarly, if you used all spiders or beads, the effect would be one of stripes. This may or may not be what you want—it would be nice for a scarf, but less satisfactory for a square shawl center.

Note, too, that the spider and the bead look very similar at a casual glance. Working these two alternately would lead to a lot of concentration in the knitting for no good effect!

Swatching like this is a very useful way to see what will work over a larger piece. And with a few knit stitches each side and knit rows each end, it makes a lovely wall hanging!

Motifs used:

1 Hexagon Frame, page 97

2 Large Diamonds, page 66

3 Bead Pattern, page 59

4 Fancy Net, page 56

5 Spider Insertion, page 73

6 Lace Hole Insertion, page 66

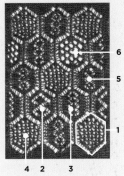

Designing with one motif in multiple ways

One of the defining qualities of Shetland lace is the way that simple motifs are used in many ways to produce different effects. By changing the spacing between repetitions of the same motif you can produce patterns that look very different from each other.

Motifs used:

1 Cat's Paw Insertion, page 65

2 Ladder Insertion, page 53

3 Cat's Paw Lace, page 72

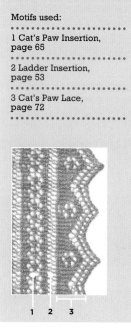

1   2   3

Insertion and lace

Here I have put the Cat's Paw Lace (page 72) together with the Cat's Paw Insertion (page 65). I've used the Ladder Insertion (page 53) on each side of the Cat's Paw Insertion to mirror the holes on the edge of the lace and to define the lace and insertion. With a couple of extra knit stitches on the straight edge, this would also make a nice scarf.

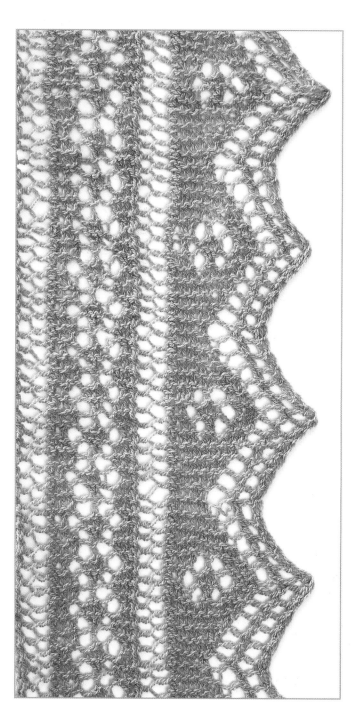

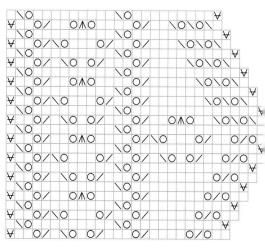

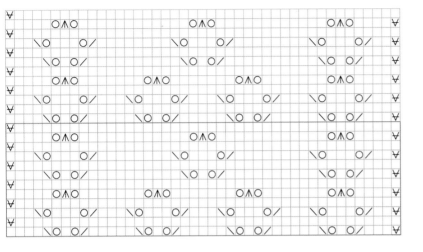

Motifs used:

1 Cat's Paw All-over,
page 77

2 Cat's Paw Insertion,
page 65

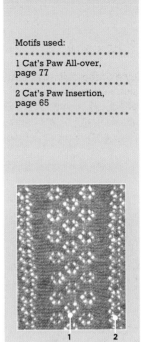

Columns and all-over

Here I have taken the Cat's Paw all-over from page 77 and added straight columns of paws on each edge. This would make a nice scarf as it is, or the "stripes" could be repeated to make a shawl center or stole. In addition, a group of four of paws would make a good filler in a shawl border.

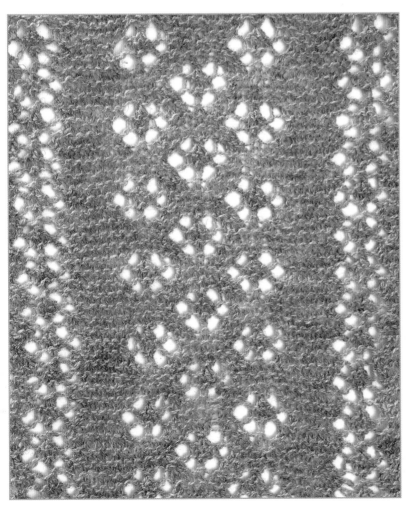

Designing a stole

When using fine yarns, it is important to make sure you have enough "solid" areas between the holes; but if these become too big the airy feel of the piece is lost. In this stole, I wanted to use the Cyprus Lace (page 89); its zigzag of holes makes the Large Diamonds (page 66) a perfect central piece. To separate them I wanted an insertion, and this needed to be edged by other, simple insertions.

As the lace and the center both use zigzag lines, I wanted a different shape for the insertion. To make my life easier I wanted something with the same row repeat, or a multiple of it. This meant 4 or 8 rows for the main insertion and 2 or 4 for the insertion to each side of it. The Bead Insertion (page 63) is a 4 row pattern with holes on every row, and it kept the airy feel but with a rounder outline. A simple steek (page 52) defines the sections without taking away from the main patterns.

I wanted the lace repeated on the opposite side of the stole. As this involves binding off stitches, the mirrored lace needed to be moved down one row.

Motifs used:

1 Cyprus Lace, page 89

2 Bead Insertion, page 63

3 Steek One, page 52

4 Large Diamonds, page 66

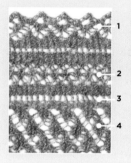

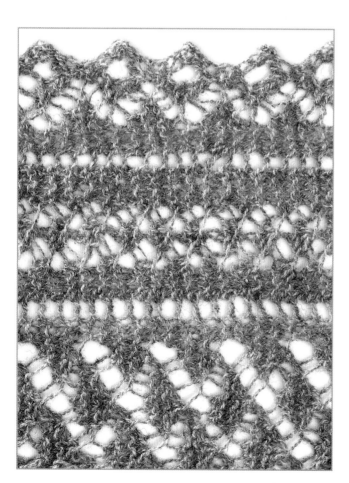

Swatch chart

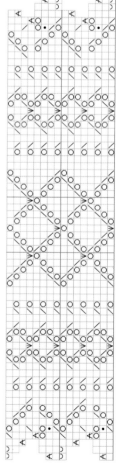

Final chart

Designing a scarf

I wanted to make a scarf with points on both sides and give the impression of stripes along the scarf. I thought I wanted insertions separated by Lace Holes (page 54), but I wasn't sure of the best spacing. As Lace Holes gives the look of lines, I wanted a "round" insertion to balance them, so I went for Eyelid Insertion (page 65), but altered it to keep all the yos on the odd-numbered rows. I used Vandyke Lace (page 61) as its double yos picked up the Lace Holes.

I wasn't sure whether a central panel of the Lace Holes Insertion (page 66) would look good, or whether the piece would have too many holes, so I swatched a panel of that as well. Once I had knitted the sample, I found that the spacing I had used worked well, but the Lace Holes Insertion didn't really fit with the ladders formed by the lace holes. Therefore, I didn't use this in the final piece.

Once I had the basic pattern spacing sorted, I needed to place the Vandyke Lace on the other side of the scarf. This involved moving the pattern down one row, so that I cast off on the beginning of a row; this has to be done when mirroring laces that use cast-off stitches. (If the shaping is just by knitting stitches together this is not necessary, as in the scarf on page 124.)

The final chart can be made any width, by altering the number of repeats of the Eyelid and Lace Holes.

Motifs used:

1 Lace Holes Insertion, page 66

2 Lace Holes, page 54

3 Eyelid Insertion, page 65

4 Vandyke Lace, page 61

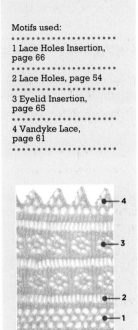

Swatch chart

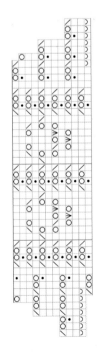

Final chart

Designing a christening gown

I wanted to design the skirt of a christening gown based on the Flee Motif (page 62), which has a 7 st, 3 or 4 row repeat (the single motif has a 3 row repeat but, when used in lines, a fourth plain row is knitted after each motif). My idea was to place flees in an all-over Hexagon Frame (page 97).

Starting with the three Flees placed above each other, I worked out the shape of the Hexagon Frame around them. This resulted in a 12 st, 24 row repeat.

I added the Cat's Paw Lace (page 72), but with the plain rows omitted, making a 12 row repeat. That wasn't wide enough, so I added the Flee Insertion (page 73) with 3 knit stitches on the straight edge. This gave a nice break between the patterns of holes.

A 12 row lace, when knitted sideways, gives 6 sts per repeat for the main pattern. That works in nicely with the 12 st repeat of the main pattern. I then added the edges for the main skirt, using 3 plain sts on each edge.

When knitting, I worked the lace first, with the first stitch of the straight edge of the lace worked as s1p so that it was easy to pick up the stitches for the main piece.

Motifs used:

1 Flee Motif, page 62

2 Hexagon Frame, page 97

3 Flee Insertion, page 73

4 Cat's Paw Lace, page 72

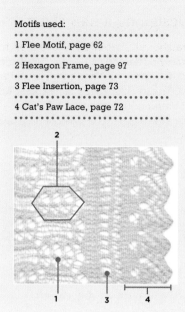

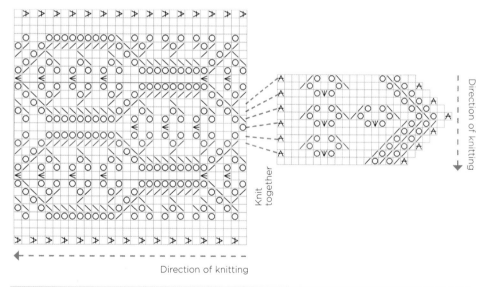

Knit together

Direction of knitting

Direction of knitting

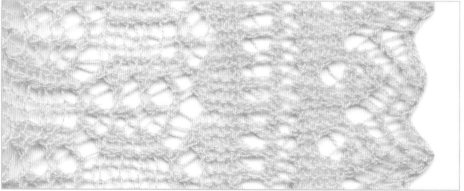

Designing a hap shawl

Traditionally, hap shawls have a plain or simply patterned center, an Old Shale border (page 108) and a lace, usually the Traditional Peaked Lace (page 106) or Brand Iron Lace (page 90). Here, I wanted to use Mrs Hunter's Pattern (page 57) for the center.

Mrs Hunter's Pattern is a 4 st, 4 row pattern but, unlike most Shetland lace patterns, the gauge does NOT result in 2 rows equaling 1 stitch. In addition, the Old Shale border has a repeat of 18 stitches, which makes the math a little tricky.

The other factor to consider is that a shawl has four corners of 90 degrees. If a border is wider than about 3in (7.5cm), to make it lie flat you have either to miter the corners, adding stitches as you go, or increase the extra stitches at the corners before you start.

This is what I did: I knitted the center square, and picked up the same number of stitches from the sides as I had cast on. I then worked out how many Old Shale repeats I had and how many stitches there were left over. Next I worked out how many stitches I needed to increase the ends of each side by, and worked these as yos on the first knit row.

The final "problem" is working out the number of lace repeats. The Traditional Peaked Lace has a 10 row repeat and Brand Iron Lace has 12. This means they reduce the border by 5 and 6 stitches per repeat. As the border has a stitch repeat of 18, i.e. 6 x 3, Brand Iron needs no further math. But the Traditional Peaked Lace does. This can be done by fudging round the corners! If the math doesn't work, always add a repeat rather than doing one less. "Miss out" decreasing a stitch from the border by working k1 at the end of the even-numbered lace rows, not knitting the last stitch together with the first of the border.

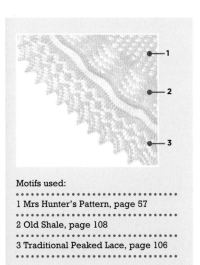

Motifs used:

1 Mrs Hunter's Pattern, page 57

2 Old Shale, page 108

3 Traditional Peaked Lace, page 106

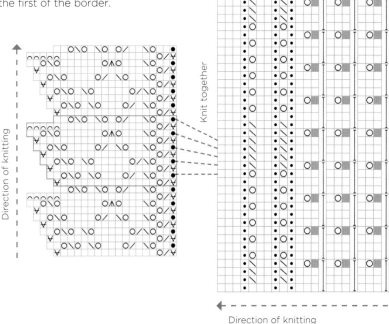

Direction of knitting

Knit together

Direction of knitting

STITCH DIRECTORY

The stitch directory opens with a stitch selector that shows all the stitches side-by-side, so that you can flick through for inspiration or quickly locate the stitch you want. It is organized into four categories: insertions, motifs, all-overs, and laces, so that if you are looking for a stitch to perform a particular function, you can survey all your options in one place. The stitch directory itself is organized by row and stitch count and includes photographs, charts, and written patterns for the stitches, as well as a number of mix-and-match suggestions.

Stitch selector

The stitch selector shows all the stitches reduced in size and side-by-side, so that you can flick through for inspiration or quickly locate the stitch you want.

ALL-OVER PATTERNS

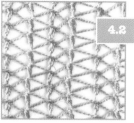
Faggotting 53

Cat's Eye 55

Bird's Eye 59

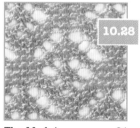
Small Diamonds 60

Arches 63

Large Diamonds 66

Acre 75

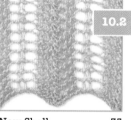
New Shell 75

Horse Shoe 76

Cat's Paw 77

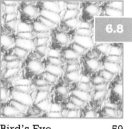
Fir Cone 83

The Madeira 84

Madeira and Diamond 85

Trellis Diamond 91

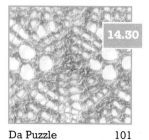
Da Puzzle 101

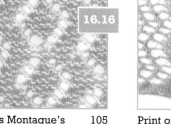
Mrs Montague's Pattern 105

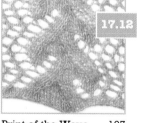
Print of the Wave 107

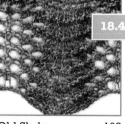
Old Shale 108

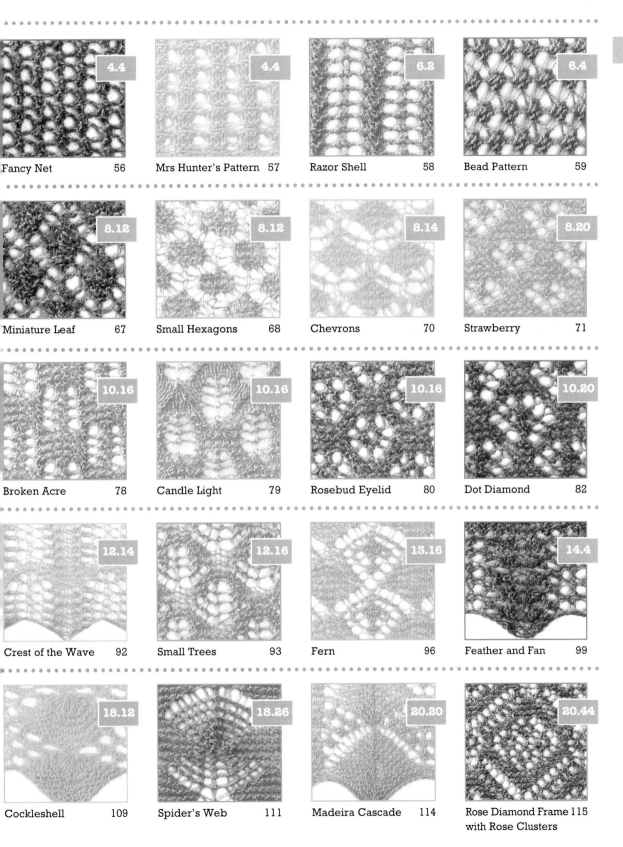

4.4 Fancy Net 56	**4.4** Mrs Hunter's Pattern 57	**6.2** Razor Shell 58	**6.4** Bead Pattern 59
8.12 Miniature Leaf 67	**8.12** Small Hexagons 68	**8.14** Chevrons 70	**8.20** Strawberry 71
10.16 Broken Acre 78	**10.16** Candle Light 79	**10.16** Rosebud Eyelid 80	**10.20** Dot Diamond 82
12.14 Crest of the Wave 92	**12.16** Small Trees 93	**13.16** Fern 96	**14.4** Feather and Fan 99
18.12 Cockleshell 109	**18.26** Spider's Web 111	**20.20** Madeira Cascade 114	**20.44** Rose Diamond Frame 115 with Rose Clusters

INSERTIONS

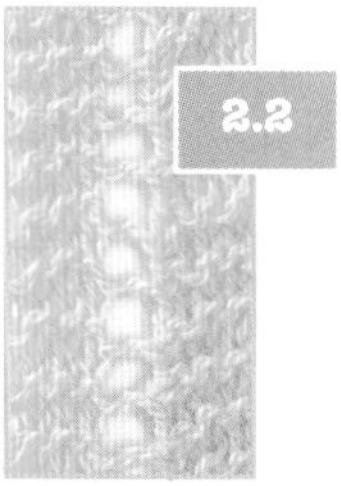

2.2
2.2
2.2

Steek One 52 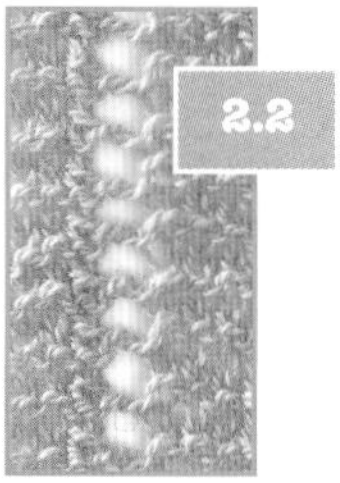 | Steek Two 52  | Steek Three 52

4.2
4.2
7.4

Ladder 53  | Lace Holes 54 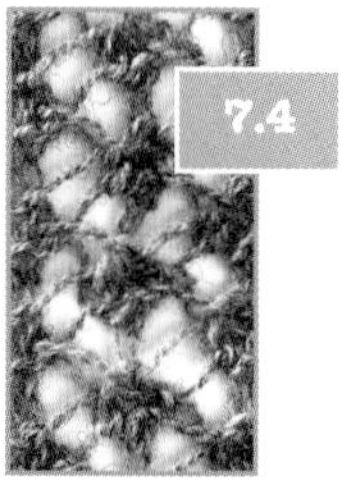 | Bead Insertion 63

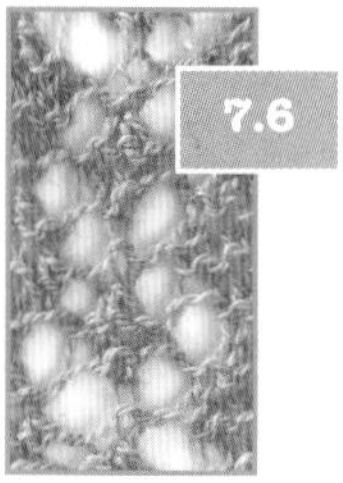

7.6
7.8
8.4

Cat's Paw Insertion 65 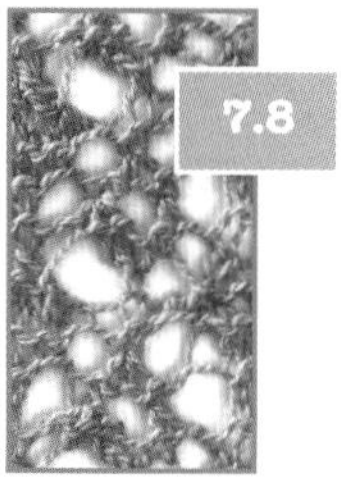 | Eyelid Insertion 65  | Lace Hole Insertion 66

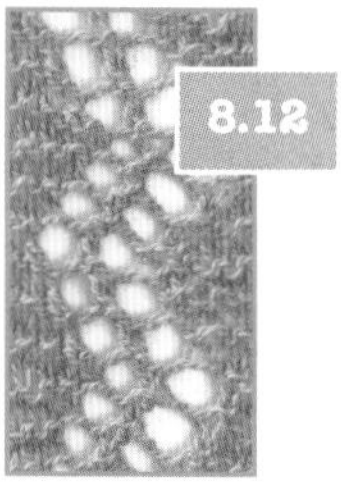

8.12
9.4
9.4

Zigzag Insertion 69 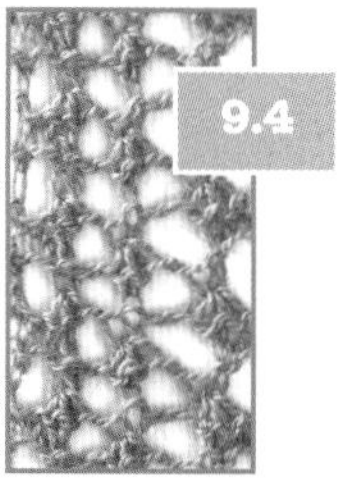 | Fancy Net 72 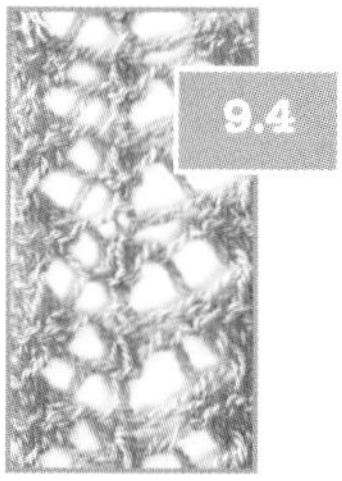 | Flee Insertion 73

9.6

Spider Insertion 73

LACE

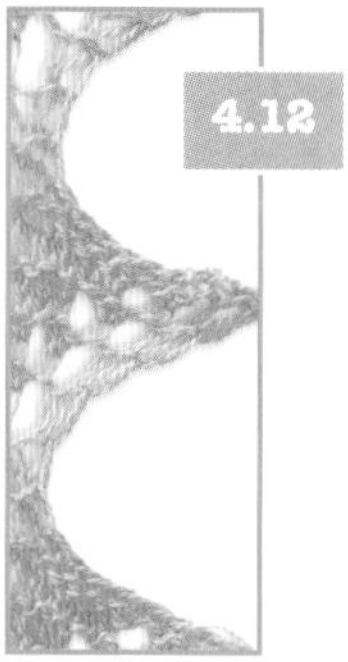

4.12
6.12
8.

Small Triangle Lace 58 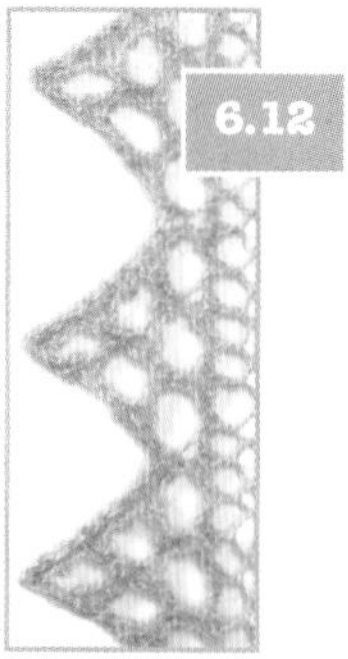 | Vandyke Lace 61 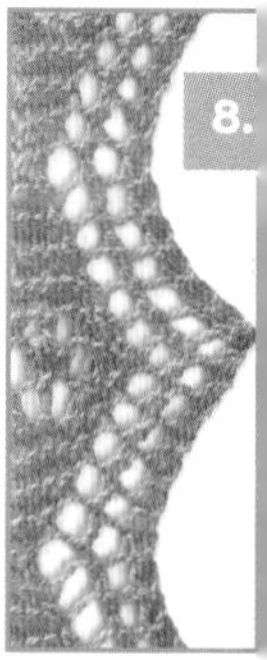 | Cat's Paw Lace

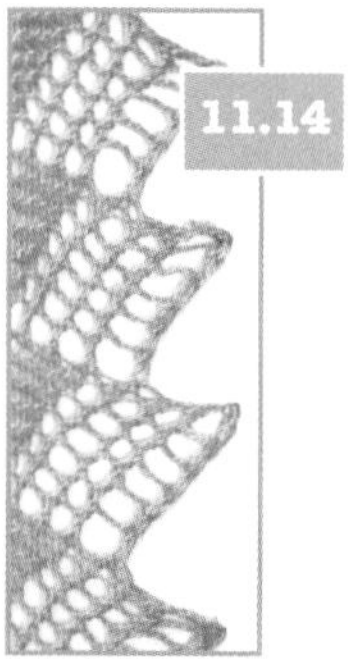

11.14
11.16
11.

Coburg Lace 86 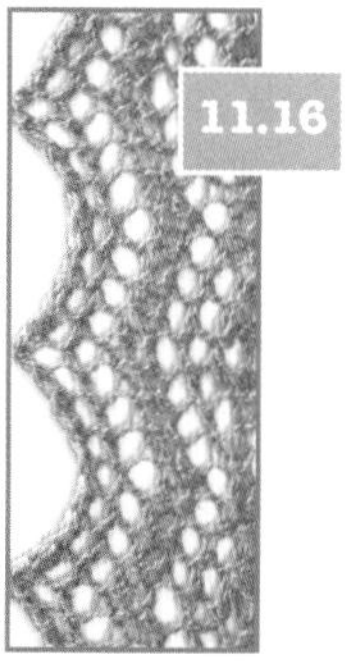 | Wave Lace 87 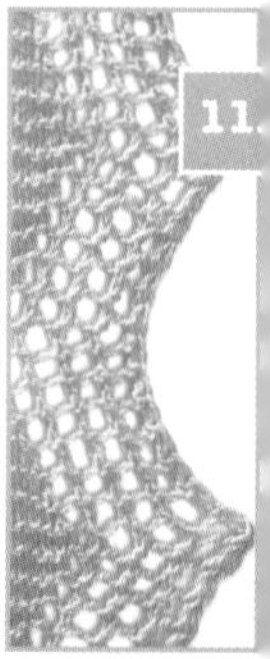 | Plain Vandyke

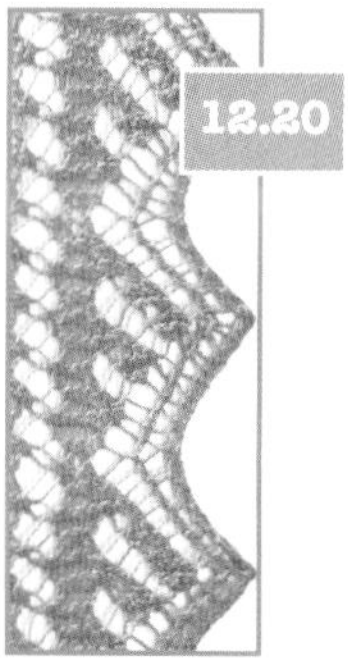

12.20
14.12
15.

Queen's Lace 94 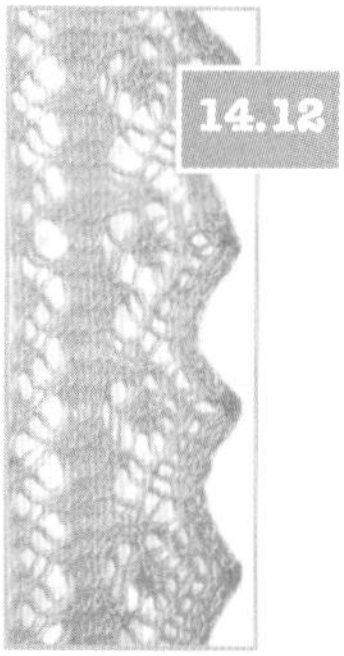 | Don's Lace 100 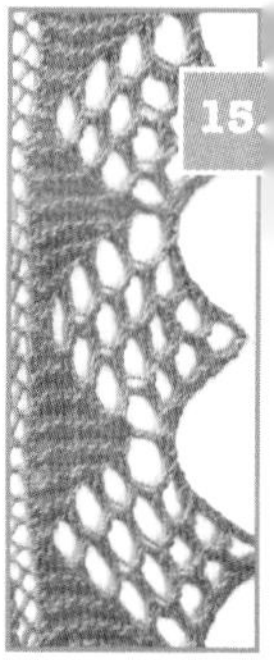 | Drops Lace

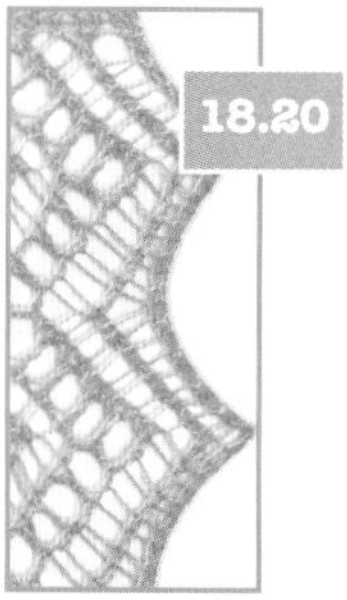

18.20
19.28
20.

Bead and Lace Holes 110 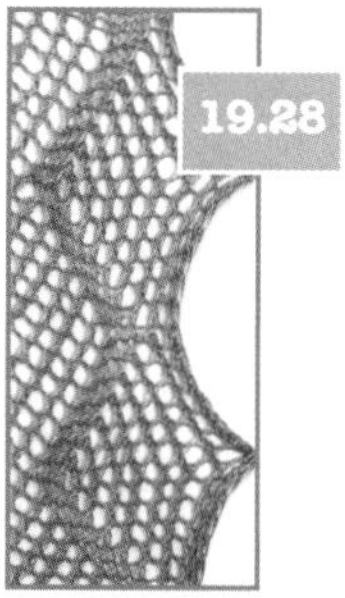 | Traditional Large Scalloped Lace 112 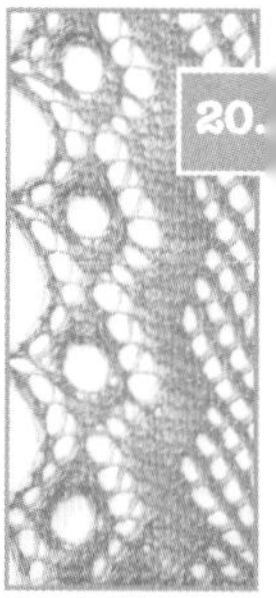 | Irish, or Elaine, Lace

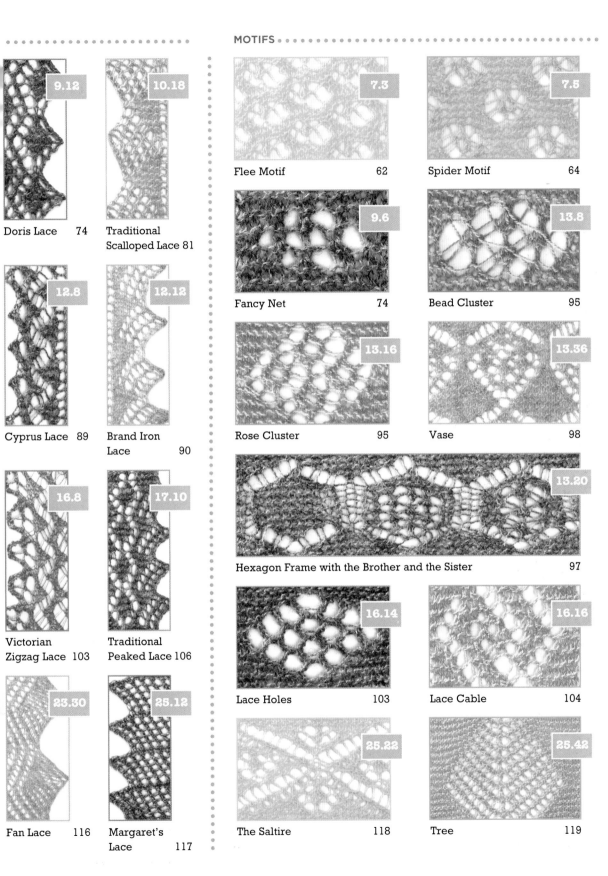

9.12

Doris Lace   74

10.18

Traditional Scalloped Lace 81

12.8

Cyprus Lace 89

12.12

Brand Iron Lace   90

16.8

Victorian Zigzag Lace 103

17.10

Traditional Peaked Lace 106

23.30

Fan Lace   116

25.12

Margaret's Lace   117

MOTIFS

7.3

Flee Motif   62

7.5

Spider Motif   64

9.6

Fancy Net   74

13.8

Bead Cluster   95

13.16

Rose Cluster   95

13.36

Vase   98

13.20

Hexagon Frame with the Brother and the Sister   97

16.14

Lace Holes   103

16.16

Lace Cable   104

25.22

The Saltire   118

25.42

Tree   119

2.2

Steek 1
▶ **INSERTION**

In Shetland, a steek is a line of holes;
there are several variations.

METHOD
Row 1: k2tog, yo
Row 2: k

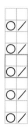

2.2

Steek 2
▶ **INSERTION**

Steeks are often used to outline other patterns or
separate sections of a bigger insertion or lace.

METHOD
Row 1: yo, ssk
Row 2: k

2.2

Steek 3
▶ **INSERTION**

This steek is the same for both rows.

METHOD
Row 1: k2tog, yo
Row 2: k2tog, yo

Ladder
▶ INSERTION

Although this has yos on every row, it is very easy to do and makes a nice break between other pattern elements. Note that the written instructions are the same for both rows.

METHOD
Row 1: k2, yo, ssk
Row 2: k2, yo, ssk

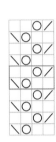

Faggotting
▶ ALL-OVER

This is Fancy Net (page 56) with the plain rows removed. It can also be used as an insertion.

METHOD
Row 1: k1, *yo, k3togtbl, yo, k1. Repeat from * to end of row
Row 2: k2tog, yo, k1, *yo, k3togtbl, yo, k1. Repeat from * to last 2 sts, yo, ssk

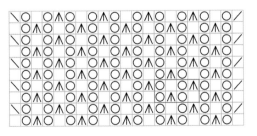

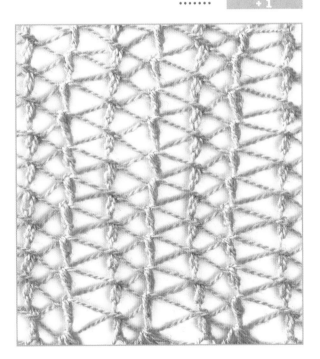

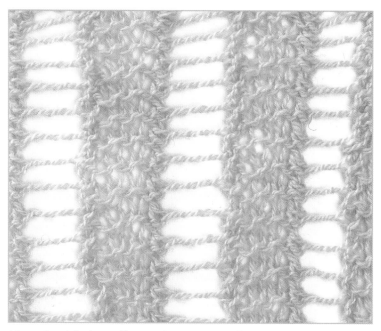

Mix-and-match shows (from top):
- Vandyke Lace, page 61
- Lace Holes, page 54
- Eyelid Insertion, page 65

For more on putting motifs together, see page 43

Lace Holes

▶ **INSERTION***

This simple little motif is used in many ways. The double yo gives a big hole which will stretch in the direction required. Note that on the second row, the second yo is usually PURLED. This makes a neater hole. If you find your hole is too big with the two yos, just do one—but remember to knit and purl into that one yo in the return row. In the sample, the right-hand column is worked with k2tog, yo, ssk; then k1, kp, k1 on the return row.

METHOD
Row 1: k2tog, yo, yo, ssk
Row 2: k2, p1, k1

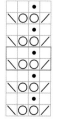

*Also features as insertion page 66, motif page 103, lace page 110

Cat's Eye

▶ ALL-OVER

Another pattern which isn't difficult but which needs concentration on the row number. It was used for shawl and stole centers and as a fill-in on shawl borders. Note that the stitch count varies between rows and that you are purling the second yo each time. Also note that the reverse side is smoother than the front.

METHOD

Row 1: k3, *yo, yo, k4. Repeat from * to last 3 sts, yo, yo, k3

Row 2: k1, *ssk, k1, p1, ssk. Repeat from * to last st, k1

Row 3: k1, *yo, k4, yo. Repeat from * to last st, k1

Row 4: k2, *ssk, ssk, k1, p1. Repeat from * to last 6 sts, ssk, ssk, k2

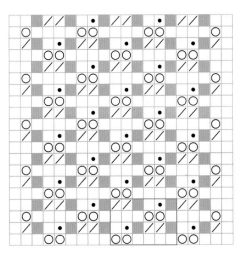

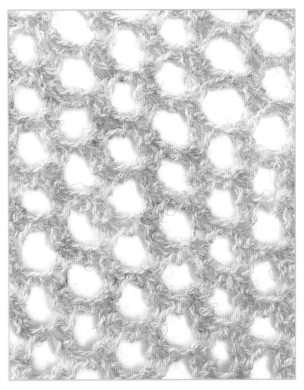

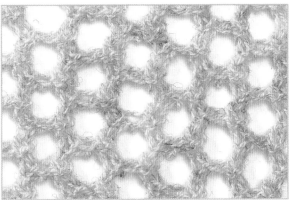

back

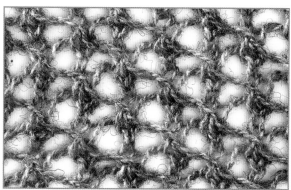

back

Fancy Net
▶ ALL-OVER*

This useful little group of stitches can be used in many ways, to form lines and shapes or as a filling. It also works well in thicker yarns on a stockinette-stitch background. Note that the reverse side is smoother than the front.

METHOD
Row 1: k1, *yo, k3togtbl, yo, k1. Repeat from * to end of row
Row 2: k
Row 3: k2tog, yo, *k1, yo, k3togtbl, yo. Repeat from * to last 3 sts, k1, yo, ssk

*Also features as insertion page 72, motif page 74

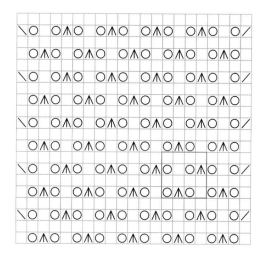

Mrs Hunter's Pattern

▶ **ALL-OVER**

This slightly unusual pattern gives a stretchy fabric.
It is useful for baby blankets in any thickness of yarn.
Note that the stitch count varies between rows.

METHOD

Row 1: k1, *s1p, k3, psso. Repeat from * to last st, k1
Row 2: k
Row 3: k1, *yo, k3. Repeat from * to last st, k1
Row 4: k

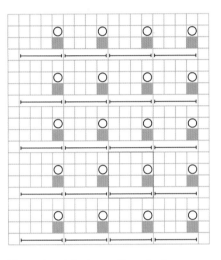

Mix-and-match shows (from top):
• Traditional Peaked Lace, page 106
• Old Shale, page 108
• Mrs Hunter's Pattern, page 57
For more on putting motifs
together, see page 45

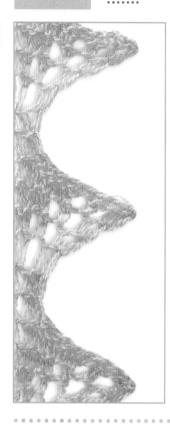

Small Triangle Lace
▶ LACE

A neat lace with sharp points. It works best edging small items; alternatively add insertions to make it wider.

METHOD
Row 1: s1p, k3
Row 2 and all alternate rows: s1p, k to end of row
Row 3: s1p, [k1, yo] twice, k1
Row 5: s1p, [k1, yo] twice, k3
Row 7: s1p, [k1, yo] twice, k5
Row 9: s1p, [k1, yo] twice, k7
Row 11: bind off 8, k to end of row
Row 12: as row 2

shown at 70%

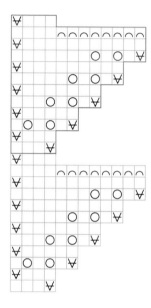

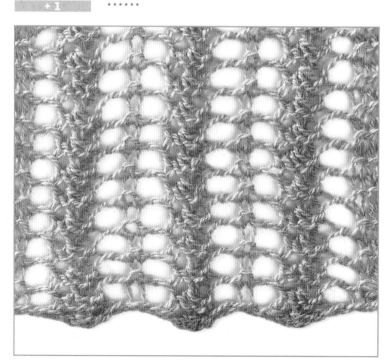

Razor Shell
▶ ALL-OVER

A small pattern which can be used as an all-over or as a single column between other patterns. The bottom edge forms small scallops.

METHOD
Row 1: *k1, yo, k1, k3togtbl, k1, yo. Repeat from * to last st, k1
Row 2: k

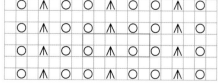

Bead Pattern

▶ **ALL-OVER***

Although there are yos on every row of this old pattern, when you knit it, you are performing basically the same actions on all odd-numbered rows and another set of actions on the even-numbered rows.

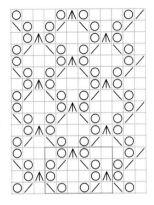

METHOD

Row 1: *k1, yo, ssk, k1, k2tog, yo.
Repeat from * to last st, k1
Row 2: *k2, yo, k3togtbl, yo, k1.
Repeat from * to last st, k1
Row 3: *k1, k2tog, yo, k1, yo, ssk.
Repeat from * to last st, k1
Row 4: k2tog, yo, *k3, yo, k3togtbl, yo.
Repeat from * to last 5 sts, k3, yo, ssk

*Also features as insertion page 63, motif page 95, lace page 110

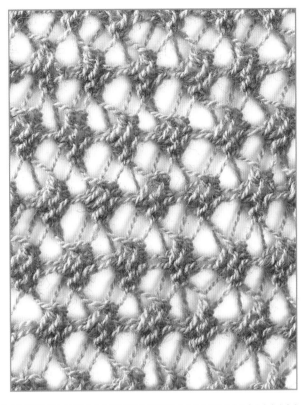

Bird's Eye

▶ **ALL-OVER**

This old pattern needs a lot of concentration! It looks best in a fine yarn, but as long as you keep an eye on the row number it isn't difficult.

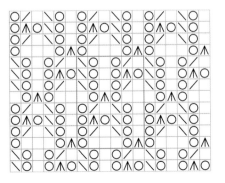

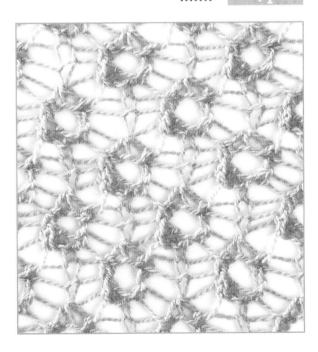

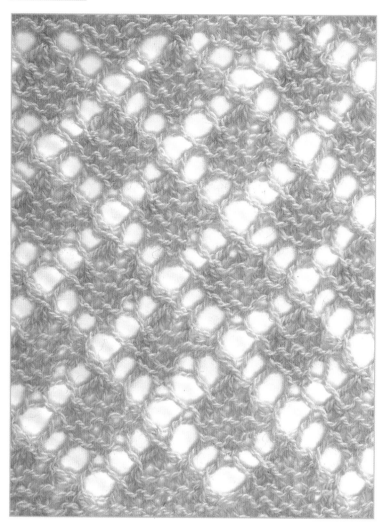

Small Diamonds
▶ **ALL-OVER**

Another simple but effective old pattern. The diamonds can easily be changed to a different size if required.

METHOD
Row 1: *k2tog, yo, k4. Repeat from * to last 3 sts, k2tog, yo, k1
Row 2 and all alternate rows: k
Row 3: k2, *yo, ssk, k1, k2tog, yo, k1. Repeat from * to last st, k1
Row 5: *k3, yo, k3togtbl, yo. Repeat from * to last 3 sts, k3
Row 7: *k3, k2tog, yo, k1. Repeat from * to last 3 sts, k3
Row 9: k2, *k2tog, yo, k1, yo, ssk, k1. Repeat from * to last st, k1
Row 11: k1, k2tog, yo, k3, *yo, k3togtbl, yo, k3. Repeat from * to last 3 sts, yo, ssk, k1
Row 12: k

Vandyke Lace

▶ LACE

This lace needs a bit of concentration to learn, but once started you see the way the holes move to give sharp points on the outer edge. The ladder insertion forms part of the overall lace. Note that row 2 starts with a yo, and that the second yo of a pair is always purled.

METHOD

Row 1: k2, yo, ssk, yo, yo, ssk
Row 2: yo, k2, p1, k2, yo, ssk
Row 3: k2, yo, ssk, k4
Row 4: k6, yo, ssk
Row 5: k2, yo, ssk, [yo, yo, ssk] twice
Row 6: [k2, p1] twice, k2, yo, ssk
Row 7: k2, yo, ssk, k6
Row 8: k8, yo, ssk
Row 9: k2, yo, ssk, [yo, yo, ssk] three times
Row 10: [k2, p1] three times, k2, yo, ssk
Row 11: k2, yo, ssk, k9
Row 12: bind off 7, k4, yo, ssk

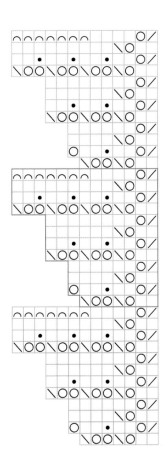

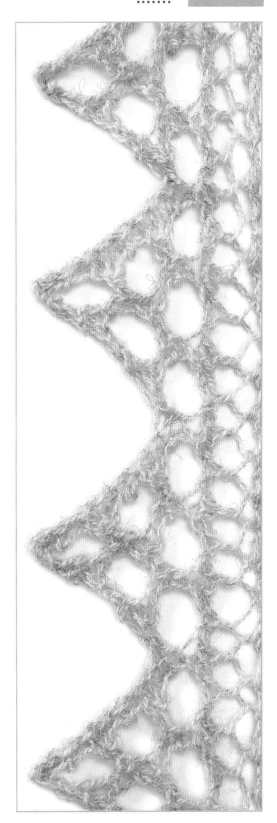

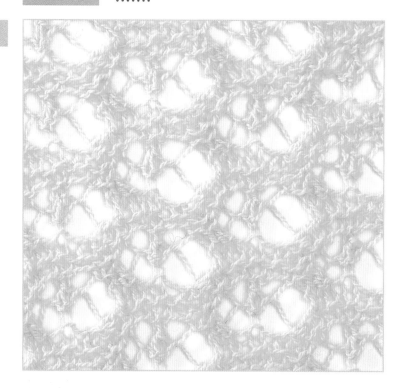

Flee Motif

▸ **MOTIF***

The basic motif is Cat's Paw without the plain rows. It can be used in "formation" to fill spaces in shawl borders, or as a lacy center. Spacing can, of course, be changed to suit.

METHOD

Row 1: *k3, k2tog, yo, k1, yo, ssk, k2. Repeat from * to last st, k1
Row 2: *k2, k2tog, yo, k3, yo, ssk, k1. Repeat from * to last st, k1
Row 3: *k4, yo, k3togtbl, yo, k3. Repeat from * to last st, k1
Row 4: k
Row 5: k5, *k3, k2tog, yo, k1, yo, ssk, k2. Repeat from * to last 6 sts, k6
Row 6: k5, *k2, k2tog, yo, k3, yo, ssk, k1. Repeat from * to last 6 sts, k6
Row 7: k5, *k4, yo, k3togtbl, yo, k3. Repeat from * to last 6 sts, k6
Row 8: k

*Also features as insertion page 73

Mix-and-match shows (from top):
• Cat's Paw Lace (omitting plain rows), page 72
• Flee Insertion, page 73
• Flee Motifs, page 62, in alternating Hexagon Frames, page 97
For more on putting motifs together, see page 44

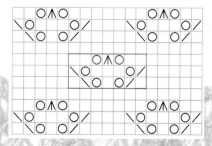

Bead Insertion

▶ **INSERTION***

A useful insertion which works best in fine yarns.

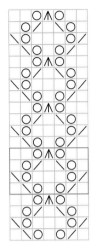

METHOD

Row 1: k1, k2tog, yo, k1, yo, ssk, k1
Row 2: k2tog, yo, k3, yo, ssk
Row 3: k1, yo, ssk, k1, k2tog, yo, k1
Row 4: k2, yo, k3togtbl, yo, k2

*Also features as all-over page 59, motif page 95, lace page 110

Arches

▶ **ALL-OVER**

This simple pattern can be seen as the "top" of a Horse Shoe (page 76). It forms a pretty, open fabric.

METHOD

Row 1: *k1, yo, k1, k3togtbl, k1, yo, k1. Repeat from * to end of row
Row 2: k
Row 3: *k2, yo, k3togtbl, yo, k2. Repeat from * to end of row
Row 4: k

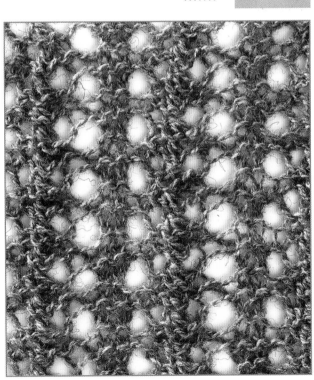

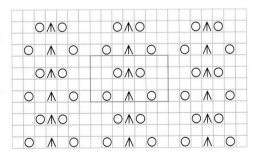

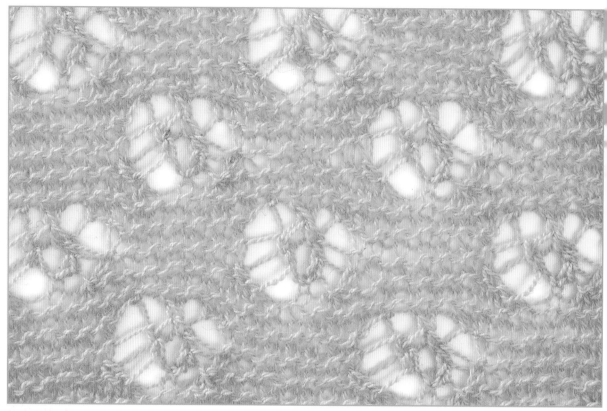

Spider Motif

▶ **MOTIF***

The group of "spider" patterns has many variations. Some have an extra row at the top, others an extra row in the middle. Note that the spider is very similar to the bead motif but with extra rows. Here I have spaced them quite widely; they work equally well closer together.

*Also features as insertion page 73

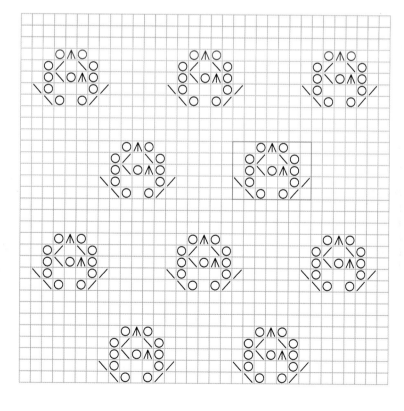

Cat's Paw Insertion

▶ INSERTION*

Another useful insertion, which goes particularly well with other patterns containing "paws."

METHOD

Row 1: k1, k2tog, yo, k1, yo, ssk, k1
Row 2: k
Row 3: k2tog, yo, k3, yo, ssk
Row 4: k
Row 5: k2, yo, k3togtbl, yo, k2, k

*Also features as lace page 72, all-over page 77

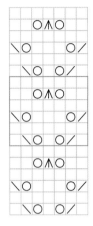

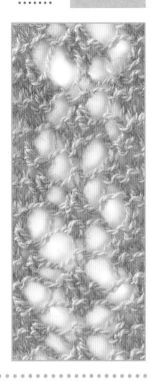

Eyelid Insertion

▶ INSERTION*

"Eyelid" is the Shetland dialect for eyelet! Single eyelids are used a lot as fillers in all kinds of items, and they can also be used as all-overs. Note that row 2 is the only even-numbered row to have yos.

METHOD

Row 1: k
Row 2: k1, k2tog, yo, k1, yo, ssk, k1
Row 3: k2tog, yo, k3, yo, ssk
Row 4: k
Row 5: k1, yo, k3togtbl, yo, k2tog, yo, k1
Row 6: k
Row 7: k2, yo, k3togtbl, yo, k2
Row 8: k

*Also features as all-over page 80

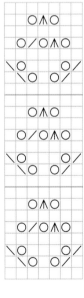

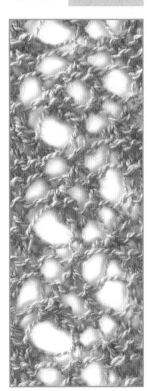

8.4

Level 1
• • • • • • •

Lace Hole Insertion
▶ INSERTION*

A useful insertion to widen the many laces which include the double yo. For a wider insertion just add multiples of 4 stitches.

METHOD
Row 1: k2, k2tog, yo, yo, ssk, k2
Row 2: k4, p1, k3
Row 3: [k2tog, yo, yo, ssk] twice
Row 4: k2, p1, k3, p1, k1

*Also features as insertion page 54, motif page 103, lace page 110

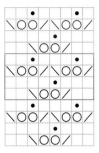

8.8
+3

Level 2
• • • • • • •

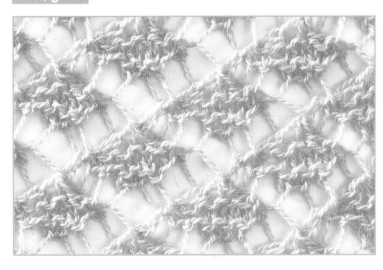

Large Diamonds
▶ ALL-OVER

Although this old pattern has yos on every row, it is very straightforward. In fine yarn it makes a lovely, elegant scarf or shawl center.

METHOD
Row 1: k2tog, yo, *k6, k2tog, yo. Repeat from * to last st, k1
Row 2: k2, *yo, ssk, k3, k2tog, yo, k1. Repeat from * to last st, k1
Row 3: k2, *k1, yo, ssk, k1, k2tog, yo, k2. Repeat from * to last st, k1
Row 4: k2, *k2, yo, k3togtbl, yo, k3. Repeat from * to last st, k1
Row 5: *k4, k2tog, yo, k2. Repeat from * to last 3 sts, k3
Row 6: *k3, k2tog, yo, k1, yo, ssk. Repeat from * to last 3 sts, k3
Row 7: k1, *k1, k2tog, yo, k3, yo, ssk. Repeat from * to last 2 sts, k2
Row 8: k1, k2tog, yo, *k5, yo, k3togtbl, yo. Repeat from * to last 8 sts, k5, yo, ssk, k1

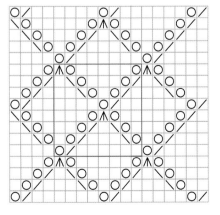

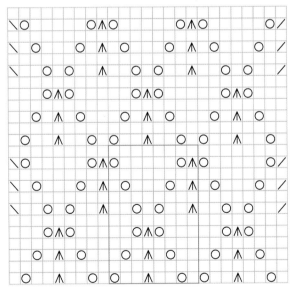

Miniature Leaf

▶ ALL-OVER

Another useful old pattern used for scarves and shawls.

METHOD

Row 1: *k1, yo, k2, k3togtbl, k2, yo. Repeat from * to last st, k1

Row 2 and all alternate rows: k

Row 3: *k2, yo, k1, k3togtbl, k1, yo, k1. Repeat from * to last st, k1

Row 5: *k3, yo, k3togtbl, yo, k2. Repeat from * to last st, k1

Row 7: k2tog, *k2, yo, k1, yo, k2, k3togtbl. Repeat from * to last 7 sts, k2, yo, k1, yo, k2, ssk

Row 9: k2tog, *k1, yo, k3, yo, k1, k3togtbl. Repeat from * to last 7 sts, k1, yo, k3, yo, k1, ssk

Row 11: k2tog, *yo, k5, yo, k3togtbl. Repeat from * to last 7 sts, yo, k5, yo, ssk

Row 12: k

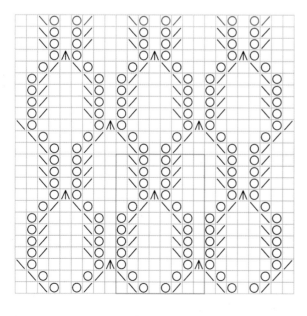

Small Hexagons

▶ ALL-OVER

This all-over pattern is a lot simpler to knit than it looks! Knitted in fine yarn it makes an elegant shawl center.

METHOD

Row 1: *k2, k2tog, yo, k1, yo, ssk, k1. Repeat from * to last st, k1

Row 2: *k1, k2tog, yo, k3, yo, ssk. Repeat from * to last st, k1

Row 3: k2tog, yo, *k5, yo, k3togtbl, yo. Repeat from * to last 7 sts, k5, yo, ssk

Rows 4 to 7: *k1, yo, ssk, k3, k2tog, yo. Repeat from * to last st, k1

Row 8: *k2, yo, ssk, k1, k2tog, yo, k1. Repeat from * to last st, k1

Row 9: *k3, yo, k3togtbl, yo, k2. Repeat from * to last st, k1

Rows 10 to 12: as row 1

Zigzag Insertion

▶ INSERTION

This insertion works well with other patterns containing wavy lines, such as Trellis Diamond (page 91). You can easily change the number of stitches and rows.

METHOD

Row 1: k2, [yo, ssk] twice, k2
Row 2 and all alternate rows: k
Row 3: k3, [yo, ssk] twice, k1
Row 5: k4, [yo, ssk] twice
Row 7: k2, [k2tog, yo] twice, k2
Row 9: k1, [k2tog, yo] twice, k3
Row 11: [k2tog, yo] twice, k4
Row 12: k

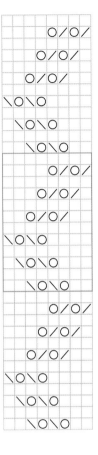

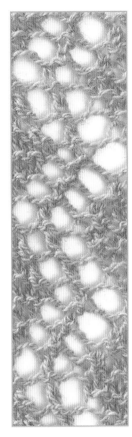

Mix-and-match shows (from top):
• Zigzag Insertion, page 69
• Eyelid Insertion, page 65

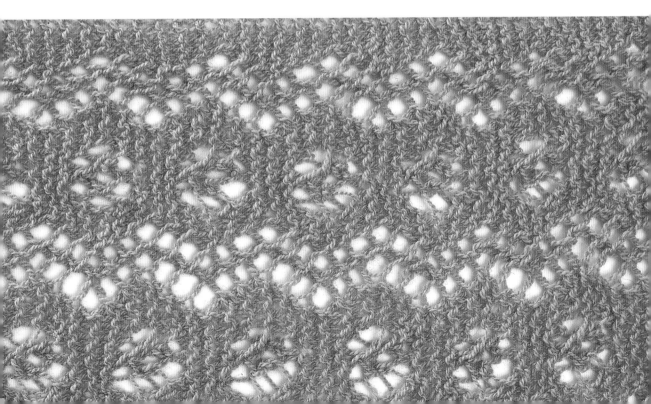

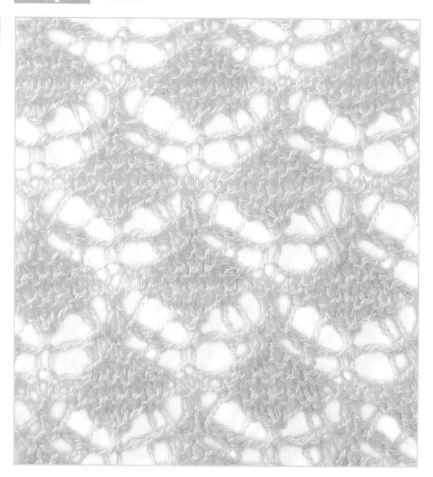

Chevrons

▶ ALL-OVER

Wavy lines can be used between other patterns, or as a pattern all of their own. You can change the number of stitches and rows easily, and their spacing. These lines also look good with plain rows between them.

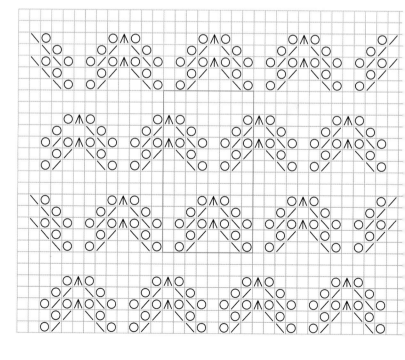

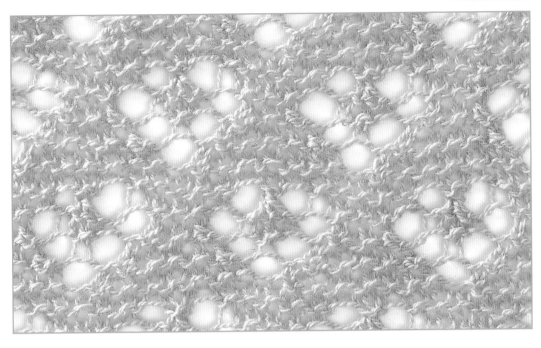

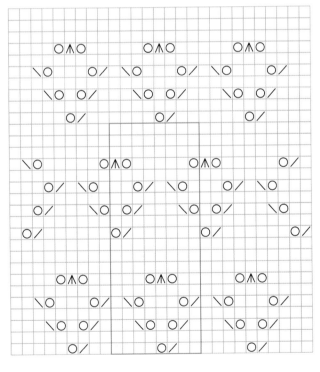

Strawberry

▶ **ALL-OVER**

This pattern is sometimes called Cat's Paw and sometimes the Strawberry. It is similar to the Strawberry motif found in the Orenberg tradition, but the decreases are slightly different.

METHOD

Row 1: k2, *k2, k2tog, yo, k4. Repeat from * to last st, k1

Row 2 and all alternate rows: k

Row 3: k2, *k1, k2tog, yo, k1, yo, ssk, k2. Repeat from * to last st, k1

Row 5: k2, *k2tog, yo, k3, yo, ssk, k1. Repeat from * to last st, k1

Row 7: k2, *k2, yo, k3togtbl, yo, k3. Repeat from * to last st, k1

Row 9: k

Row 11: *k2tog, yo, k6. Repeat from * to last 3 sts, k2tog, yo, k1

Row 13: k1, *k1, yo, ssk, k3, k2tog, yo. Repeat from * to last 2 sts, k2

Row 15: k1, *k2, yo, ssk, k1, k2tog, yo, k1. Repeat from * to last 2 sts, k2

Row 17: k1, k2tog, yo, k5, *yo, k3togtbl, yo, k5. Repeat from * to last 3 sts, yo, ssk, k1

Row 19: k

Row 20: k

8.24   Level 1
• • • • • •

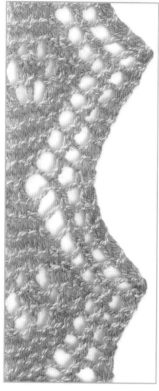

shown at 70%

Cat's Paw Lace
▶ **LACE***

The perfect lace for an item which includes cat's paws! For a wider lace, add the Cat's Paw Insertion (page 65).

METHOD
Row 1: k2, yo, k2tog, yo, k4
Row 2 and all alternate rows: k
Row 3: k2, yo, k2tog, yo, k5
Row 5: k2, yo, k2tog, yo, k6
Row 7: k2, yo, k2tog, yo, k7
Row 9: k2, yo, k2tog, yo, k2, k2tog, yo, k1, yo, ssk, k1
Row 11: k2, yo, k2tog, yo, k2, k2tog, yo, k3, yo, ssk
Row 13: k1, [ssk, yo] twice, ssk, k2, yo, k3togtbl, yo, k2
Row 15: k1, [ssk, yo] twice, ssk, k6
Row 17: k1, [ssk, yo] twice, ssk, k5
Row 19: k1, [ssk, yo] twice, ssk, k4
Row 21: k1, [ssk, yo] twice, ssk, k3
Row 23: k1, [ssk, yo] twice, ssk, k2
Row 24: as row 2

*Also features as insertion page 65, all-over page 77

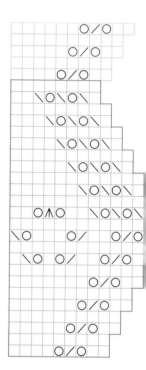

9.4   Level 1
• • • • •

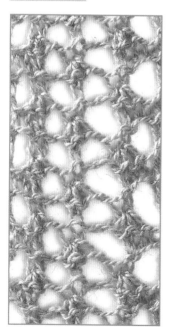

Fancy Net
▶ **INSERTION***

A useful little insertion which gives an open area between the border and the lace.

METHOD
Row 1: k3, yo, k3togtbl, yo, k3
Row 2: k
Row 3: [k1, yo, k3togtbl, yo] twice, k1
Row 4: k

*Also features as all-over page 56, motif page 74

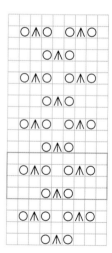

Flee Insertion
▸ **INSERTION***

Da Flee is Shetland dialect for "the fly," as the holes in this motif look like fly's wings. It forms a useful, lacy insertion.

METHOD
Row 1: k2, k2tog, yo, k1, yo, ssk, k2
Row 2: k1, k2tog, yo, k3, yo, ssk, k1
Row 3: k3, yo, k3togtbl, yo, k3
Row 4: k

*Also features as motif page 62

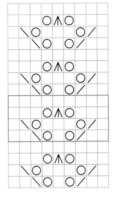

Spider Insertion
▸ **INSERTION***

When worked as an insertion, the spider motif has the effect of a string of round holes between the center and the lace. Keep an eye on which row you are on, and remember the knit row between the spiders!

*Also features as motif page 64, all-over page 77

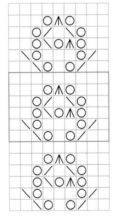

9.6 Level 1

Fancy Net
▶ MOTIF*

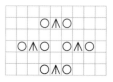

Groups of Fancy Net can be used in many places. They can be any size and shape, and were often used in large zigzags, or as frames for other motifs.

METHOD
Row 1: k3, yo, k3togtbl, yo, k3
Row 2 and all alternate rows: k
Row 3: k1, [yo, k3togtbl, yo, k1] twice
Row 5: as row 1
Row 6: k

*Also features as all-over page 57, insertion page 72

9.12 Level 1

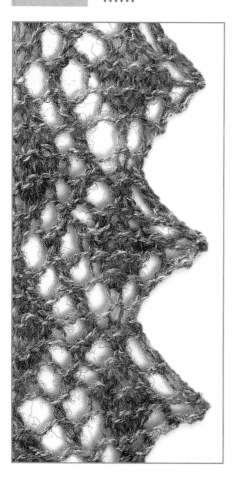

Doris Lace
▶ LACE

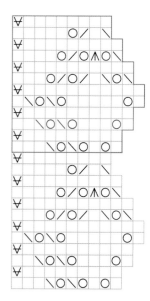

This simple lace is effective in all yarn weights and in garter or stockinette stitch. Note that it has only one stitch outside the yo on the outer edge.

METHOD
Row 1: [k1, yo] twice, [ssk, yo] twice, k3
Row 2 and all alternate rows: s1p, k to end of row
Row 3: k1, yo, k3, [yo, ssk] twice, k2
Row 5: k1, yo, k5, [yo, ssk] twice, k1
Row 7: ssk, yo, ssk, k1, [k2tog, yo] twice, k3
Row 9: ssk, yo, k3togtbl, yo, k2tog, yo, k4
Row 11: ssk, k1, k2tog, yo, k5
Row 12: s1p, k to end of row

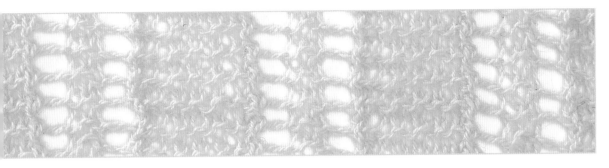

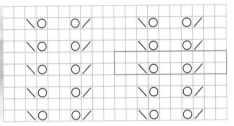

Acre

▶ **ALL-OVER**

An old pattern used for "hosiery" i.e. gloves, scarves and hats as well as stockings. Worked on a stockinette-stitch background it is still good for socks today!

METHOD

Row 1: *k2, k2tog, yo, k2, yo, ssk, k2. Repeat from * to end of row
Row 2: k

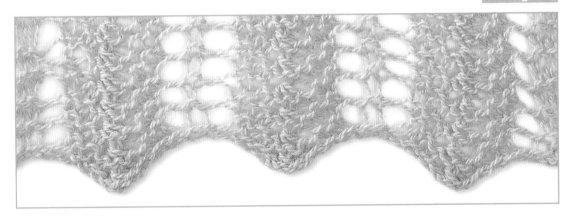

New Shell

▶ **ALL-OVER**

Another old pattern. It gives a scalloped edge, and looks good with changing colors.

METHOD

Row 1: *k1, yo, k3, k3togtbl, k3, yo. Repeat from * to last st, k1
Row 2: k

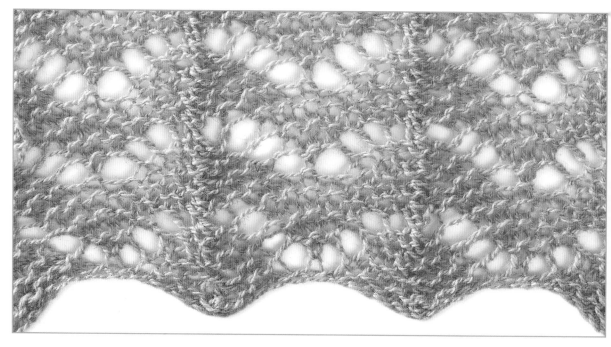

Horse Shoe

▶ ALL-OVER

A very useful old pattern which works well in all weights of yarn and on stockinette- or garter-stitch backgrounds.

METHOD

Row 1: k2tog, k3, yo, *k1, yo, k3, k3togtbl, k3, yo. Repeat from * to last 6 sts, k1, yo, k3, ssk

Row 2 and all alternate rows: k

Row 3: k2tog, k2, yo, k1, *k2, yo, k2, k3togtbl, k2, yo, k1. Repeat from * to last 6 sts, k2, yo, k2, ssk

Row 5: k2tog, k1, yo, k2, *k3, yo, k1, k3togtbl, k1, yo, k2. Repeat from * to last 6 sts, k3, yo, k1, ssk

Row 7: k2tog, yo, k3, *k4, yo, k3togtbl, yo, k3. Repeat from * to last 6 sts, k4, yo, ssk

Row 8: k

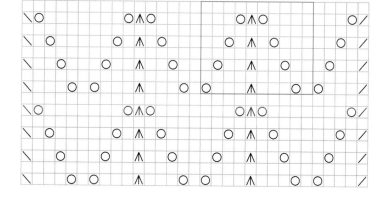

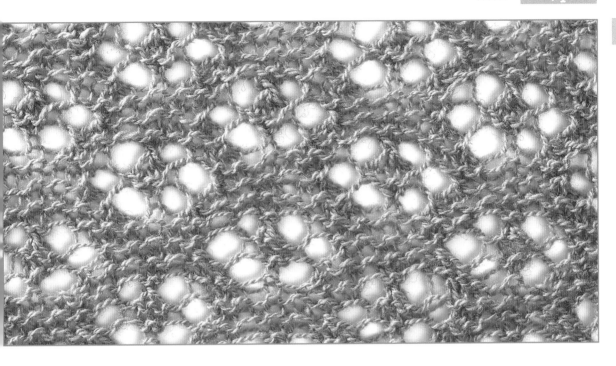

Cat's Paw

▶ **ALL-OVER***

The Cat's Paw motif can be placed in many different ways—in "stripes" with or without plain stitches between, or staggered as shown here. It can be used in any yarn in garter or stockinette stitch, alone or in "clumps." It is an invaluable weapon in the Shetland lace knitter's armory!

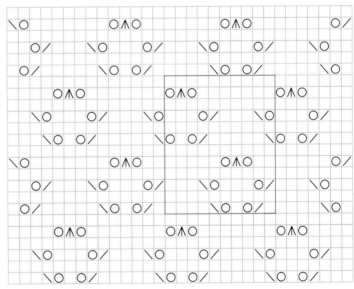

METHOD

Row 1: *k3, k2tog, yo, k1, yo, ssk, k2. Repeat from * to last st, k1

Row 2 and all alternate rows: k

Rows 3: *k2, k2tog, yo, k3, yo, ssk, k1. Repeat from * to last st, k1

Row 5: *k4, yo, k3togtbl, yo, k3. Repeat from * to last st, k1

Row 7: k1, yo, ssk, k2, *k3, k2tog, yo, k1, yo, ssk, k2. Repeat from * to last 6 sts, k3, k2tog, yo, k1

Row 9: k2, yo, ssk, k1, *k2, k2tog, yo, k3, yo, ssk, k1. Repeat from * to last 6 sts, k2, k2tog, yo, k2

Row 11: k2tog, yo, k3, *k4, yo, k3togtbl, yo, k3. Repeat from * to last 6 sts, k4, yo, ssk

Row 12: k

*Also features as insertion page 65, lace page 72

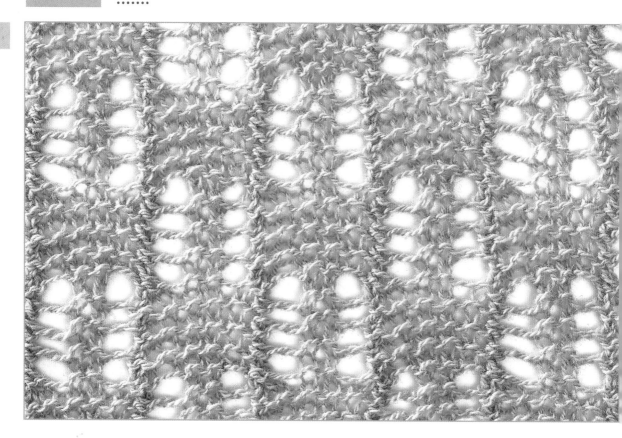

Broken Acre

▶ **ALL-OVER**

This version of the Acre pattern makes a very easy and pretty scarf or center to a shawl. It works equally well on a garter- or stockinette-stitch background in any weight of yarn.

METHOD

Row 1: k1, yo, ssk, k2, *k2, k2tog, yo, k2, yo, ssk, k2. Repeat from * to last 5 sts, k2, k2tog, yo, k1

Row 2: k

Rows 3 to 8: repeat rows 1 and 2 three times more

Row 9: *k2, k2tog, yo, k2, yo, ssk, k2. Repeat from * to end of row

Row 10: k

Rows 11 to 16: repeat rows 9 and 10 three times more

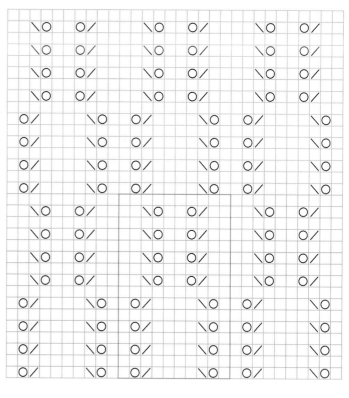

Candle Light

▶ **ALL-OVER**

This pretty pattern needs a bit more concentration than many with yos only on odd-numbered rows. In thicker yarns it looks best worked on a stockinette-stitch background to highlight the diamond lines of the decreases.

METHOD

Row 1: *k3, k2tog, yo, k1, yo, ssk, k2. Repeat from * to last st, k1

Row 2 and all alternate rows: k

Row 3: *k2, k2tog, k1, yo, k1, yo, k1, ssk, k1. Repeat from * to last st, k1

Row 5: *k1, k2tog, k2, yo, k1, yo, k2, ssk. Repeat from * to last st, k1

Row 7: k2tog, k3, yo, k1, yo, k3, *k3togtbl, k3, yo, k1, yo, k3. Repeat from * to last 2 sts, ssk

Row 9: *k1, yo, ssk, k5, k2tog, yo. Repeat from * to last st, k1

Row 11: *k1, yo, k1, ssk, k3, k2tog, k1, yo. Repeat from * to last st, k1

Row 13: *k1, yo, k2, ssk, k1, k2tog, k2, yo. Repeat from * to last st, k1

Row 15: *k1, yo, k3, k3togtbl, k3, yo. Repeat from * to last st, k1

Row 16: k

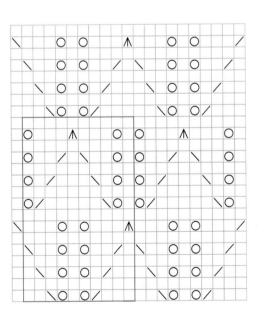

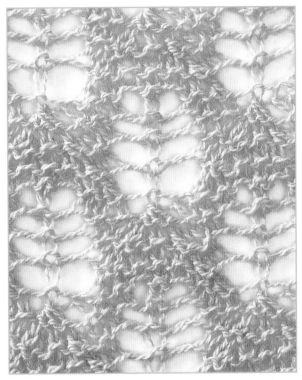

Garter-stitch background

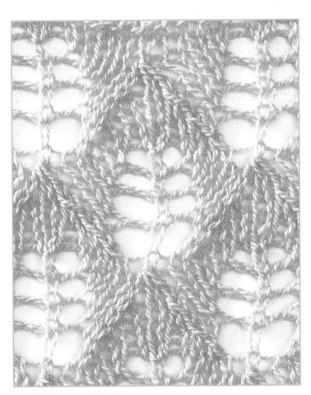

Stockinette-stitch background

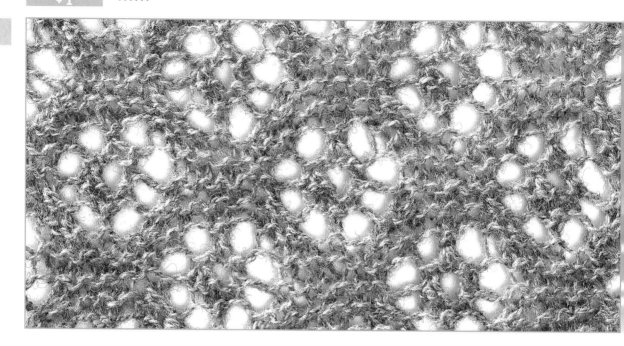

Rosebud Eyelid

▶ **ALL-OVER***

An "eyelid" (eyelet) pattern. Note that this is the same sequence of stitches as the Spider, but with plain rows between the patterned ones. This motif can be used as an insertion as well as an all-over and, as an all-over, the eyelids can be positioned either close together for an open effect or with more stitches between.

METHOD

Row 1: *k3, k2tog, yo, k1, yo, ssk, k2. Repeat from * to last st, k1

Row 2 and all alternate rows: k

Row 3: *k2, k2tog, yo, k3, yo, ssk, k1. Repeat from * to last st, k1

Row 5: *k3, yo, ssk, yo, k3togtbl, yo, k2. Repeat from * to last st, k1

Row 7: *k4, yo, k3togtbl, yo, k3. Repeat from * to last st, k1

Row 9: k1, yo, ssk, k2, *k3, k2tog, yo, k1, yo, ssk, k2. Repeat from * to last 6 sts, k3, k2tog, yo, k1

Row 11: k2, yo, ssk, k1, *k2, k2tog, yo, k3, yo, ssk, k1. Repeat from * to last 6 sts, k2, k2tog, yo, k2

Row 13: k1, k2tog, yo, k2, *k3, yo, ssk, yo, k3togtbl, yo, k2. Repeat from * to last 6 sts, k3, yo, ssk, k1

Row 15: k2tog, yo, k3, *k4, yo, k3togtbl, yo, k3. Repeat from * to last 6 sts, k4, yo, ssk

Row 16: k

*Also features as insertion page 65

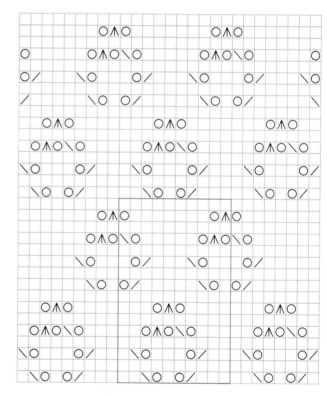

Traditional Scalloped Lace

▶ **LACE**

A lace often used on the edge of hap shawls. It can be made bigger or smaller very easily by adding or subtracting rows in the center.

METHOD

Row 1: k1, k2tog, yo, k5, yo, k2
Row 2 and all alternate rows: sl1p, k to end of row
Row 3: k1, k2tog, yo, k4, yo, ssk, yo, k2
Row 5: k1, k2tog, yo, k3, [yo, ssk] twice, yo, k2
Row 7: k1, k2tog, yo, k2, [yo, ssk] three times, yo, k2
Row 9: k1, k2tog, yo, k1, [yo, ssk] four times, yo, k2
Row 11: k1, k2tog, yo, k1, k2tog, [yo, k2tog] four times, k1
Row 13: k1, k2tog, yo, k2, k2tog, [yo, k2tog] three times, k1
Row 15: k1, k2tog, yo, k3, k2tog, [yo, k2tog] twice, k1
Row 17: k1, k2tog, yo, k4, k2tog, yo, k2tog, k1
Row 18: k

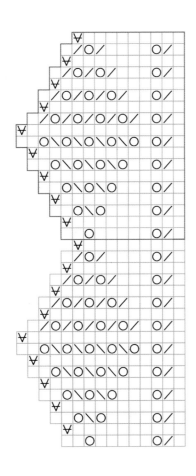

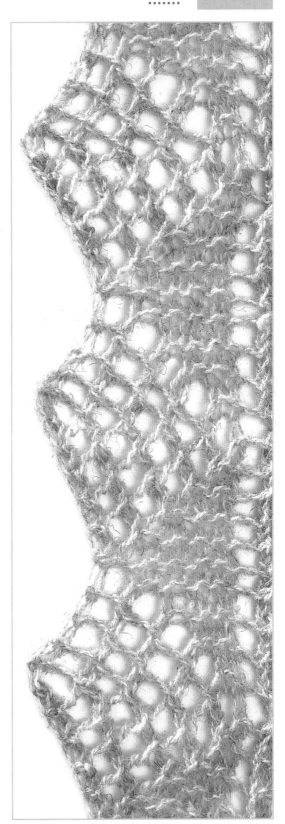

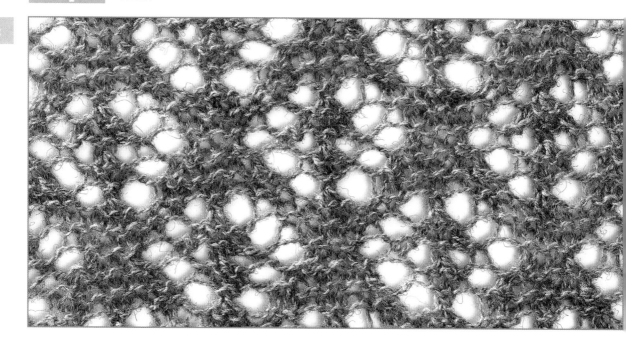

Dot Diamond

▶ ALL-OVER

I found this pattern on a couple of very old pieces in Unst. I don't know if it has a name! It makes a simple and effective shawl center.

METHOD

Row 1: *k4, yo, k3togtbl, yo, k3. Repeat from * to last st, k1

Row 2 and all alternate rows: k

Row 3: *k2, k2tog, yo, k3, yo, ssk, k1. Repeat from * to last st, k1

Row 5: *k1, k2tog, yo, k1, yo, k3togtbl, yo, k1, yo, ssk. Repeat from * to last st, k1

Row 7: *k3, yo, ssk, k1, k2tog, yo, k2. Repeat from * to last st, k1

Row 9: as row 1

Row 11: k2tog, yo, k7, *yo, k3togtbl, yo, k7. Repeat from * to last 2 sts, yo, ssk

Row 13: k2, yo, ssk, k3, *k2tog, yo, k3, yo, ssk, k3. Repeat from * to last 4 sts, k2tog, yo, k2

Row 15: k2tog, yo, k1, yo, ssk, *k1, k2tog, yo, k1, yo, k3togtbl, yo, k1, yo, ssk. Repeat from * to last 6 sts, k1, k2tog, yo, k1, yo, ssk

Row 17: k1, k2tog, yo, k5, *yo, ssk, k1, k2tog, yo, k5. Repeat from * to last 3 sts, yo, ssk, k1

Row 19: as row 11

Row 20: k

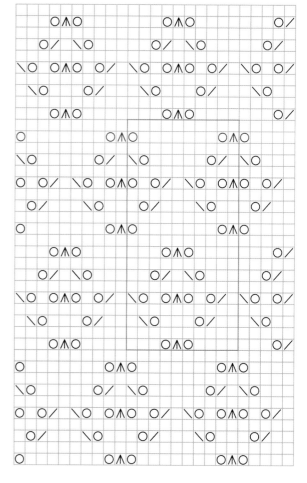

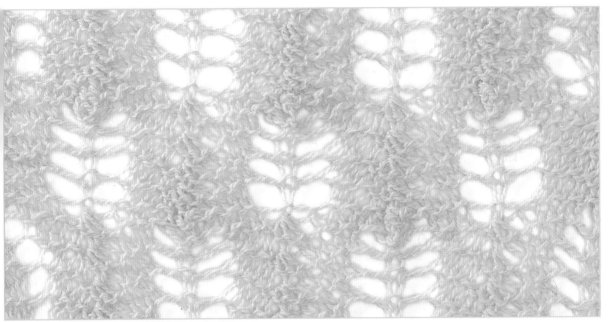

Fir Cone

▶ **ALL-OVER**

This simple pattern forms "pockets" as you knit then, when it is dressed, the tops of the fir cones flatten and form the rounded shapes. Note that the basic pattern row is the same as New Shell (page 75) and the first row of Horse Shoe (page 76).

METHOD

Row 1: k2tog, k3, yo, *k1, yo, k3, k3tbl, k3, yo. Repeat from * to last 6 sts, k1, yo, k3, ssk

Row 2: k

Rows 3 to 10: repeat rows 1 and 2 four times more

Row 11: k1, *yo, k3, k3tbl, k3, yo, k1. Repeat from * to end of row

Row 12: k

Rows 13 to 20: repeat rows 11 and 12 four times more

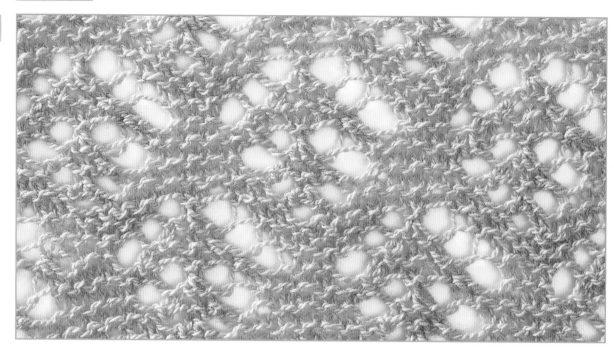

The Madeira

▶ **ALL-OVER**

This pattern was very popular in the nineteenth century and you can see it used in many pieces and photographs. It could have been taken originally from a Spanish shawl, but we don't know.

METHOD

Row 1: *k4, k2tog, yo, k4. Repeat from * to last st, k1
Row 2 and all alternate rows: k
Row 3: *k4, yo, k3togtbl, yo, k3. Repeat from * to last st, k1
Row 5: *k3, yo, ssk, k1, k2tog, yo, k2. Repeat from * to last st, k1
Row 7: as row 3
Row 9: *k2, yo, ssk, k3, k2tog, yo, k1. Repeat from * to last st, k1
Row 11: as row 5
Row 13: as row 3
Row 15: k5, *k4, k2tog, yo, k4. Repeat from * to last 6 sts, k6
Row 17: k2tog, yo, k3, *k4, yo, k3togtbl, yo, k3. Repeat from * to last 6 sts, k4, yo, ssk
Row 19: k1, k2tog, yo, k2, *k3, yo, ssk, k1, k2tog, yo, k2. Repeat from * to last 6 sts, k3, yo, ssk, k1
Row 21: as row 17
Row 23: k2, k2tog, yo, k1, *k2, yo, ssk, k3, k2tog, yo, k1. Repeat from * to last 6 st, k2, yo, ssk, k2
Row 25: as row 19
Row 27: as row 17

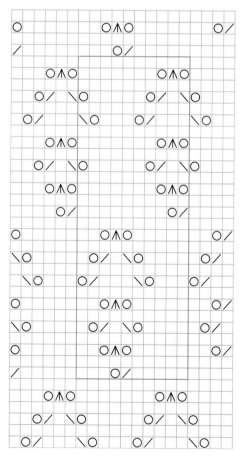

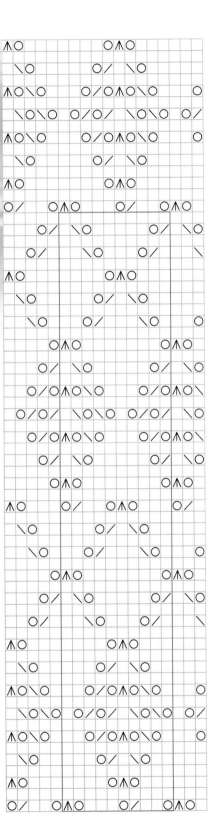

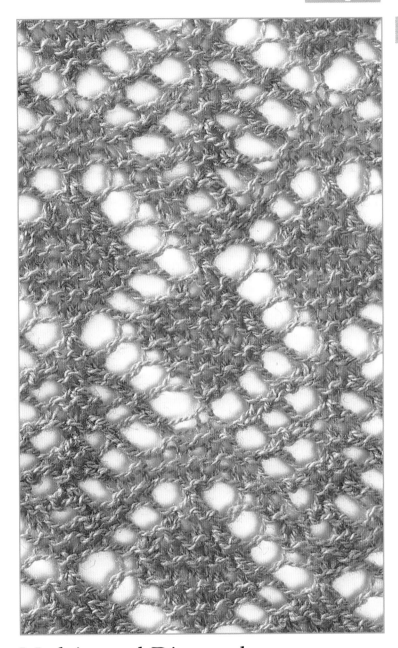

Madeira and Diamond

▶ ALL-OVER

This asymmetric pattern is quite common on old pieces. The repeat as shown makes a nice shawl border. Note that the "madeira" here is not the same as "The Madeira!"

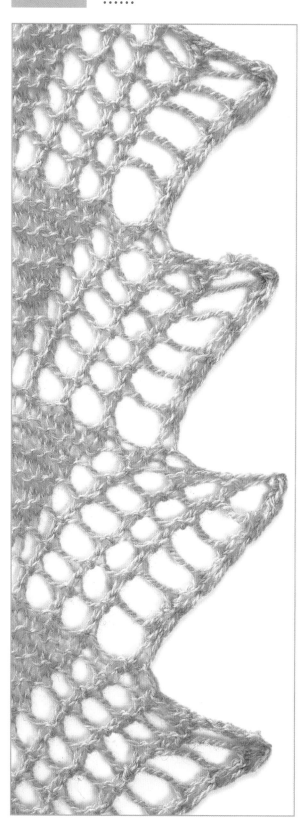

Coburg Lace
▶ LACE

This old lace differs from Brand Iron (page 90) as it has the large lace holes at its outer edge instead of a single hole.

METHOD

Row 1: s1p, k2tog, [yo] twice, [k2tog, yo] three times, k2

Row 2: s1p, k8, p1, k2

Row 3: s1p, k2tog, [yo] twice, [k2tog, yo] three times, k3

Row 4: s1p, k9, p1, k2

Row 5: s1p, k2tog, [yo] twice, [k2tog, yo] three times, k4

Row 6: s1p, k10, p1, k2

Row 7: s1p, k2tog, [yo] twice, [k2tog, yo] three times, k5

Row 8: s1p, k11, p1, k2

Row 9: s1p, k2tog, [yo] twice, [k2tog, yo] three times, k6

Row 10: s1p, k12, p1, k2

Row 11: s1p, k2tog, [yo] twice, [k2tog, yo] three times, k7

Row 12: s1p, k13, p1, k2

Row 13: bind off 6, k to end of row

Row 14: s1p, k10

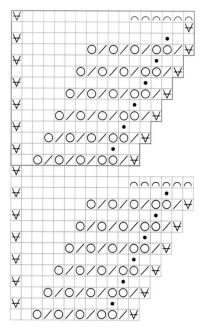

Wave Lace

▶ **LACE**

This is a smaller, narrower version of the Traditional Scalloped Lace (page 81). If you are not confident starting the alternate rows with the yo, ssk, then use s1p, k1 instead.

METHOD

Row 1: k3, yo, ssk, k2, yo, ssk, yo, k2
Row 2 and all alternate rows: yo, ssk, k to end of row
Row 3: k2, [yo, ssk] twice, k2, yo, ssk, yo, k2
Row 5: k3, [yo, ssk] twice, k2, yo, ssk, yo, k2
Row 7: k2, [yo, ssk] three times, k2, yo, ssk, yo, k2
Row 9: k2, [k2tog, yo] twice, k2, [k2tog, yo] twice, k2tog, k1
Row 11: k1, [k2tog, yo] twice, k2, [k2tog, yo] twice, k2tog, k1
Row 13: k2, k2tog, yo, k2, [k2tog, yo] twice, k2tog, k1
Row 15: k1, k2tog, yo, k2, [k2tog, yo] twice, k2tog, k1
Row 16: yo, ssk, k to end of row

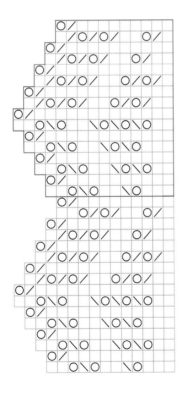

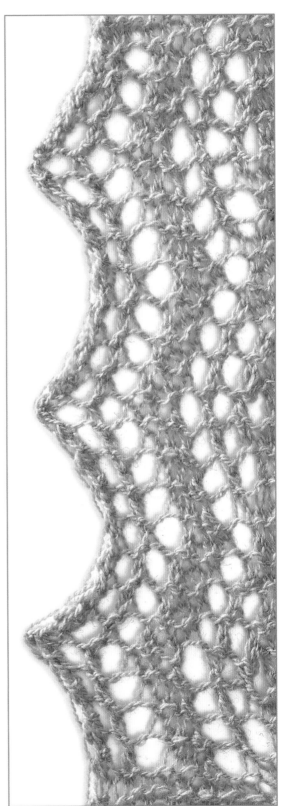

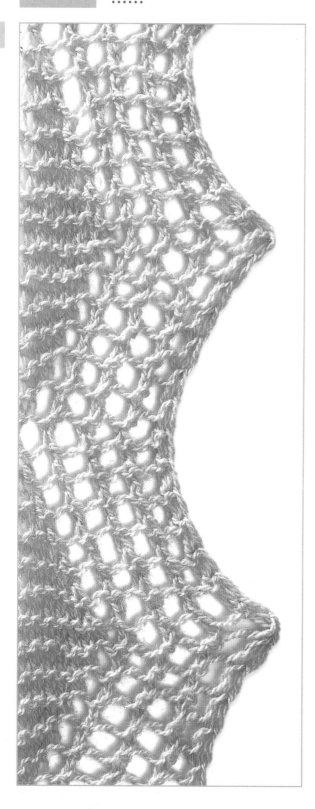

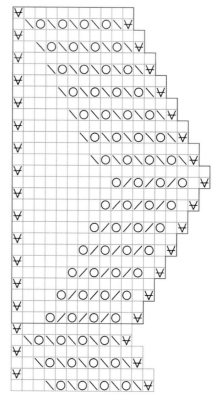

Plain Vandyke
▶ **LACE**

This useful edging is easy to do and very versatile. You can alter both the number of yo lines and the number of rows in the pattern very easily.

METHOD

Row 1: s1p, k1, [yo, k2tog] three times, yo, k3
Row 2 and all alternate rows: s1p, k to end of row
Row 3: s1p, k1, [yo, k2tog] three times, yo, k4
Row 5: s1p, k1, [yo, k2tog] three times, yo, k5
Row 7: s1p, k1, [yo, k2tog] three times, yo, k6
Row 9: s1p, k1, [yo, k2tog] three times, yo, k7
Row 11: s1p, k1, [yo, k2tog] three times, yo, k8
Row 13: s1p, k1, [yo, k2tog] three times, yo, k9
Row 15: s1p, [ssk, yo] four times, ssk, k7
Row 17: s1p, [ssk, yo] four times, ssk, k6
Row 19: s1p, [ssk, yo] four times, ssk, k5
Row 21: s1p, [ssk, yo] four times, ssk, k4
Row 23: s1p, [ssk, yo] four times, ssk, k3
Row 25: s1p, [ssk, yo] four times, ssk, k2
Row 27: s1p, [ssk, yo] four times, ssk, k1
Row 28: s1p, k to end of row

Cyprus Lace

▶ **LACE**

This old pattern is one which has to be learnt by heart! Study the chart before you start it. But the work is worth it—it is a dainty edging which works best in fine yarns.

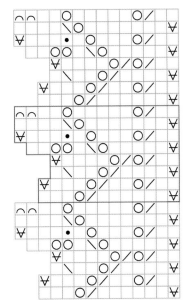

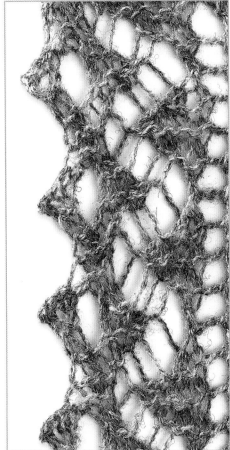

Mix-and-match shows (from top):
- Cyprus Lace, page 89
- Steek One, page 52
- Bead Insertion, page 63
- Steek One, page 52
- Large Diamonds, page 66

For more on putting motifs together, see page 42

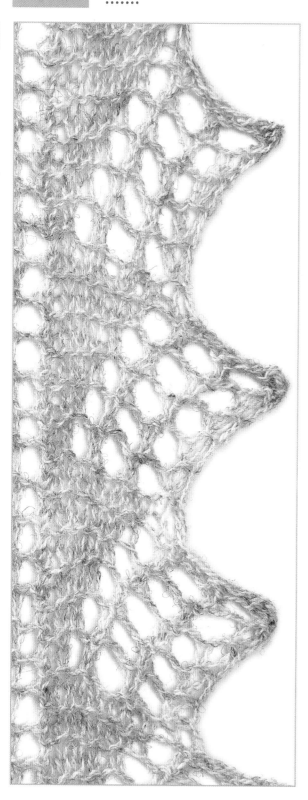

Brand Iron Lace

▶ LACE

A common, old pattern which is very useful. This is one of the easiest edgings which works well in any yarn.

METHOD

Row 1: s1p, k1, [yo, k2tog] twice, yo, k1, k2tog, yo, k3
Row 2 and all alternate rows: s1p, k to end of row
Row 3: s1p, k1, [yo, k2tog] twice, yo, k2, k2tog, yo, k3
Row 5: s1p, k1, [yo, k2tog] twice, yo, k3, k2tog, yo, k3
Row 7: s1p, k1, [yo, k2tog] twice, yo, k4, k2tog, yo, k3
Row 9: s1p, k1, [yo, k2tog] twice, yo, k5, k2tog, yo, k3
Row 11: bind off 5, k7, k2tog, yo, k3
Row 12: s1p, k to end of row

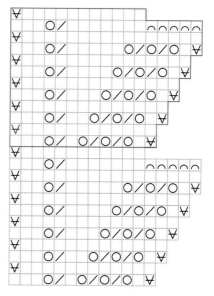

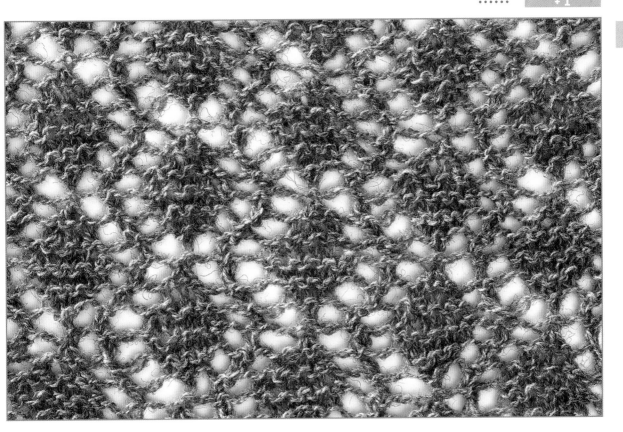

Trellis Diamond

▶ ALL-OVER

If you look at the lines of yos in this pattern you will see how you can adapt it to have three or more lines of yos, or longer "zigs" and "zags."

METHOD

Row 1: k1, *k1, [k2tog, yo] twice, k1, [yo, ssk] twice, k2. Repeat from * to end of row

Row 2 and all alternate rows: k

Row 3: k1, *[k2tog, yo] twice, k3, [yo, ssk] twice, k1. Repeat from * to end of row

Row 5: k2tog, *yo, k2tog, yo, k5, yo, ssk, yo, k3togtbl. Repeat from * to last 11 sts, yo, k2tog, yo, k5, [yo, ssk] twice

Row 7: k1, *[yo, ssk] twice, k3, [k2tog, yo] twice, k1. Repeat from * to end of row

Row 9: k1, *k1, [yo, ssk] twice, k1, [k2tog, yo] twice, k2. Repeat from * to end of row

Row 11: k1, *k2, yo, ssk, yo, k3togtbl, yo, k2tog, yo, k3. Repeat from * to end of row

Row 12: k

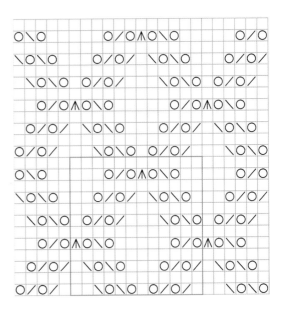

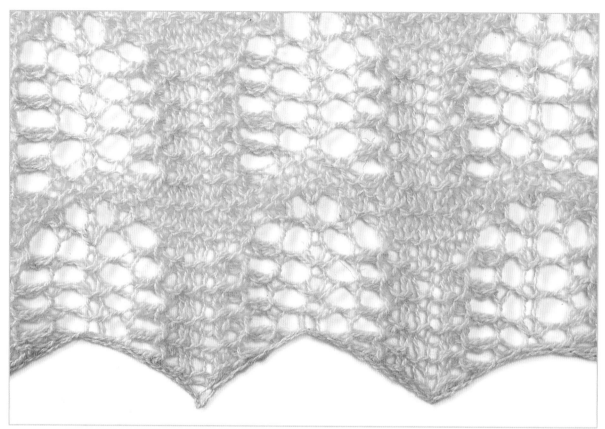

Crest of the Wave

▶ ALL-OVER

A pretty pattern which forms scallops at its edge.
It can be used instead of Old Shale as a border for
shawls. It can also be knitted with rows 1 to 10 on a
stockinette-stitch background and rows 11 to 14 in
garter stitch.

METHOD

Row 1: *k1, k2tog twice, [yo, k1] three times, yo,
ssk twice. Repeat from * to last st, k1
Row 2: k
Rows 3 to 10: repeat rows 1 and 2 four times more
Rows 11 to 14: k

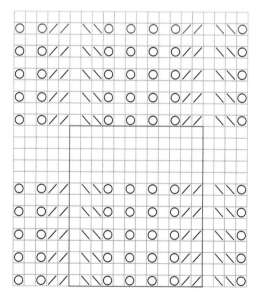

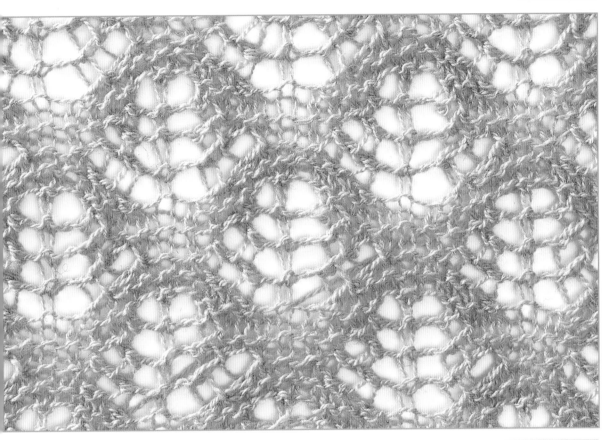

Small Trees

▶ **ALL-OVER**

Trees come in all sizes! Here they are spaced fairly close, and staggered. Their size and spacing can be changed to suit.

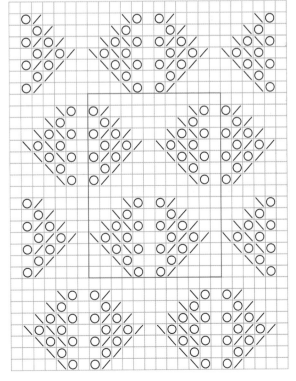

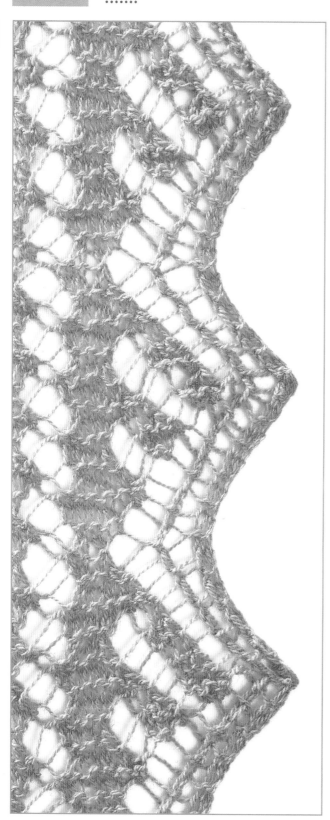

Queen's Lace

▶ LACE

An old lace with deep points which makes a lovely lace for a shawl with zigzags or diamonds in the design.

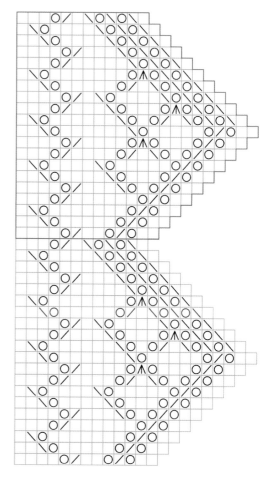

Bead Cluster

▶ MOTIF*

Another motif which can be made bigger if required. It fills in gaps in borders nicely!

METHOD

Row 1: k4, k2tog, yo, k1, yo, ssk, k4
Row 2: k3, k2tog, yo, k3, yo, ssk, k3
Row 3: [k1, k2tog, yo, k1, yo, ssk] twice, k1
Row 4: k2tog, yo, k3, yo, k3togtbl, yo, k3, yo, ssk
Row 5: [k1, yo, ssk, k1, k2tog, yo] twice, k1
Row 6: [k2, yo, k3togtbl, yo, k1] twice, k1
Row 7: k4, yo, ssk, k1, k2tog, yo, k4
Row 8: k5, yo, k3togtbl, yo, k5

*Also features as all-over page 59, insertion page 63, lace page 110

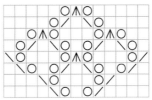

Rose Cluster

▶ MOTIF

Here the Rose motif has been joined to make a cluster. You can easily increase the size by adding extra segments.

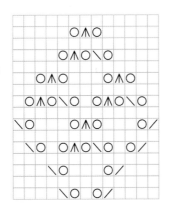

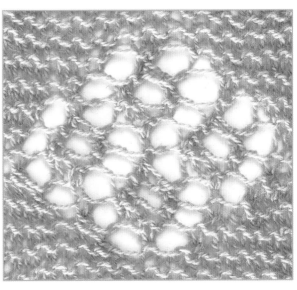

METHOD

Row 1: k4, k2tog, yo, k1, yo, ssk, k4
Row 2 and all alternate rows: k
Row 3: k3, k2tog, yo, k3, yo, ssk, k3
Row 5: k1, k2tog, yo, k1, yo, ssk, yo, k3togtbl, yo, k1, yo, ssk, k1
Row 7: k2tog, yo, k3, yo, k3togtbl, yo, k3, yo, ssk
Row 9: [k1, yo, ssk, yo, k3togtbl, yo] twice, k1
Row 11: [k2, yo, k3togtbl, yo, k1] twice, k1
Row 13: k4, yo, ssk, yo, k3togtbl, yo, k4
Row 15: k5, yo, k3togtbl, yo, k5
Row 16: k

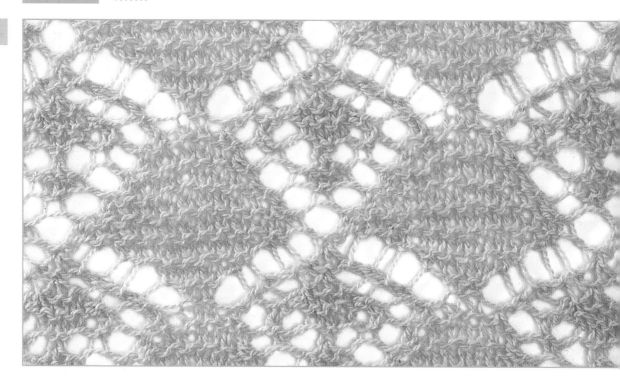

Fern

▶ ALL-OVER

This pattern gives a lovely contrast between lacy and plain areas of fabric.

METHOD

Row 1: *k5, k2tog, yo, k6. Repeat from * to end of row
Rows 2, 4, 6, 8, 10: k
Row 3: *k4, k2tog, yo, k1, yo, ssk, k4. Repeat from * to end of row
Row 5: *k3, k2tog, yo, k3, yo, ssk, k3. Repeat from * to end of row
Row 7: *k2, k2tog, yo, k1, yo, k3togtbl, yo, k1, yo, ssk, k2. Repeat from * to end of row
Row 9: *k1, [k2tog, yo] twice, k3, [yo, ssk] twice, k1
Row 11: *k1, [yo, ssk] twice, k3, [k2tog, yo] twice, k1. Repeat from * to end of row
Row 12: *k2, [yo, ssk] twice, k1, [k2tog, yo] twice, k2. Repeat from * to end of row
Row 13: *k3, yo, ssk, yo, k3togtbl, yo, k2tog, yo, k3. Repeat from * to end of row
Row 14: *k4, yo, ssk, k1, k2tog, yo, k4. Repeat from * to end of row
Row 15: *k5, yo, k3togtbl, yo, k5. Repeat from * to end of row
Row 16: k

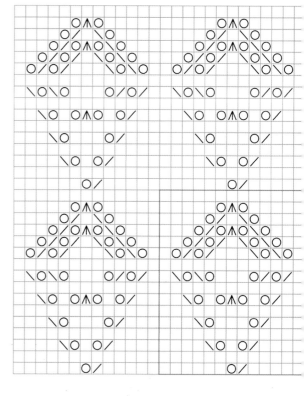

shown at 75%

Hexagon Frame with the Brother and the Sister

▶ MOTIF

The Brother (center) and the Sister (right) are well-known motifs, often used alternately in shawl borders and stole ends. If you look closely, you can see that the Brother has Fancy Net (page 74) in the hexagon frame while the Sister has Beads (page 95). Note that although the center pattern looks to be too far down in the frame, when knitted it appears central. The hexagon frame can be used to enclose other design elements, and its exact size can easily be altered.

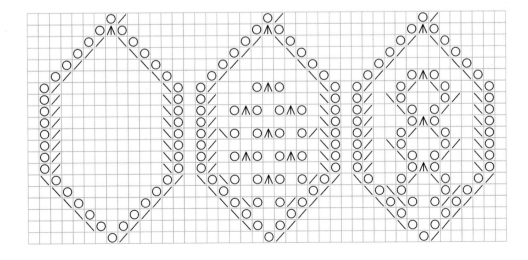

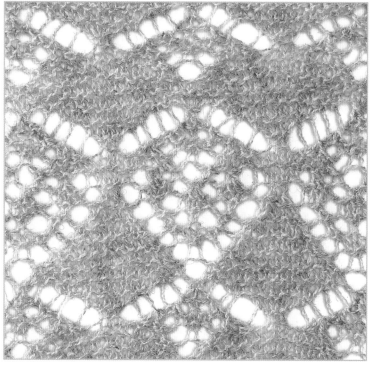

shown at 60%

Vase
▶ MOTIF

I found this on a shawl in a photo on the Shetland Museum and Archives site. It makes a nice end to a scarf or stole, and is straightforward to knit.

METHOD

Row 1: *k5, k2tog, yo, k6. Repeat from * to end of row

Rows 2, 4, 6, 8, 10, 12, 14, 16: k

Row 3: *k4, k2tog, yo, k1, yo, ssk, k4. Repeat from * to end of row

Row 5: *k3, k2tog, yo, k3, yo, ssk, k3. Repeat from * to end of row

Row 7: *k2, [k2tog, yo] twice, k1, [yo, ssk] twice, k2. Repeat from * to end of row

Row 9: *k1, [k2tog, yo] twice, k3, [yo, ssk] twice, k1. Repeat from * to end of row

Row 11: *k2tog, yo, k3, yo, k3togtbl, yo, k3, yo, ssk. Repeat from * to end of row

Row 13: *k2, yo, k3togtbl, yo, k2tog, yo, k1, yo, k3togtbl, yo, k2. Repeat from * to end of row

Row 15: as row 3

Row 17: *k1, yo, ssk, k2tog, yo, k3, yo, ssk, k2tog, yo, k1. Repeat from * to end of row

Row 18: *k2, yo, ssk, k5, k2tog, yo, k2. Repeat from * to end of row

Row 19: *k3, yo, k3togtbl, yo, k1, yo, k3togtbl, yo, k3. Repeat from * to end of row

Row 20: *k4, yo, ssk, k1, k2tog, yo, k4. Repeat from * to end of row

Row 21: *k5, yo, k3togtbl, yo, k5. Repeat from * to end of row

Rows 22 to 26: k

Row 27: as row 1

Rows 28 to 36: as rows 14 to 22

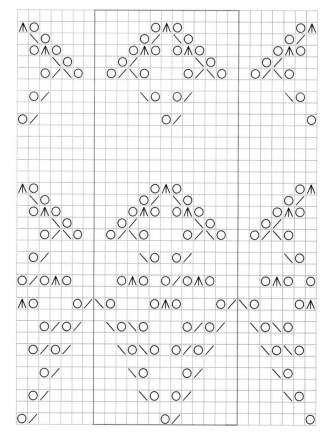

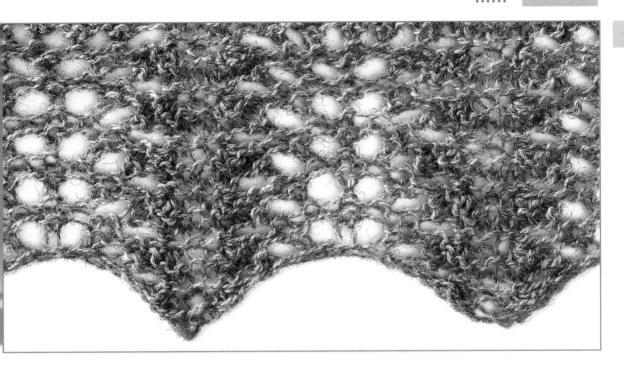

Feather and Fan

▶ **ALL-OVER**

This is the stitch Shetlanders call Feather and Fan! It has steeper decreases than Old Shale (page 108), and forms deeper scallops.

METHOD

Row 1: *k1, k4tog, [yo, k1] five times, yo, k4togtbl. Repeat from * to last st, k1

Rows 2 to 4: k

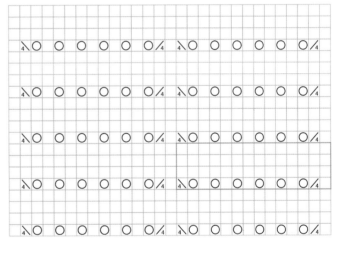

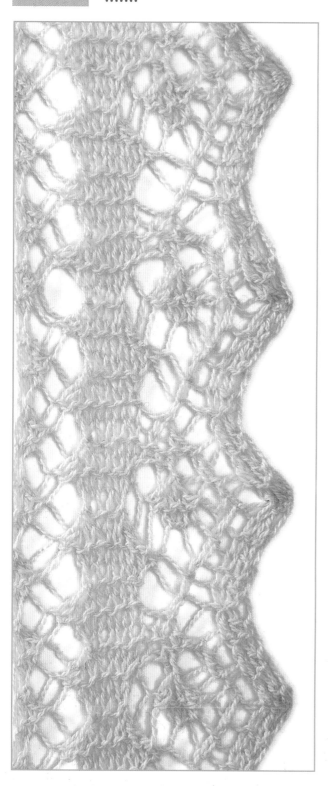

Don's Lace

▶ LACE

This lace is a smaller version of Queen's Lace (page 94). It looks best in finer yarns. Note that the inner seven stitches form an insertion which could be used on its own.

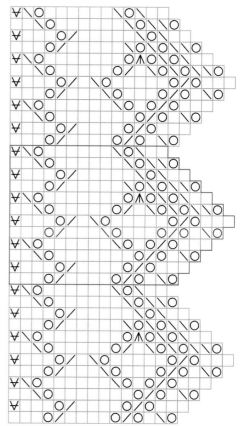

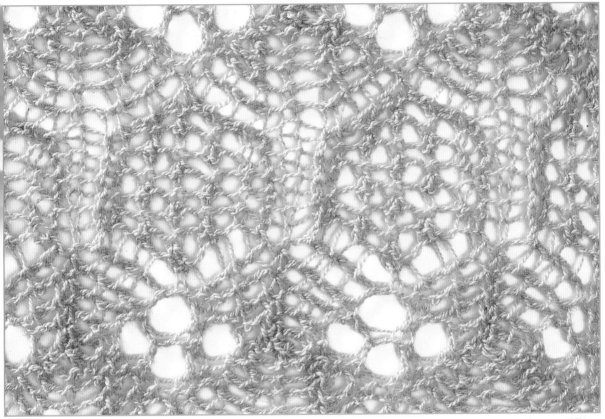

shown at 75%

Da Puzzle

▶ **ALL-OVER**

This is a shawl center used in the very finest shawls in Unst. At first sight it looks daunting, but if you break it down, each part is straightforward. The pattern repeat is only 14 sts, so the sequence is easily remembered; there are only a few rows where you really have to concentrate.

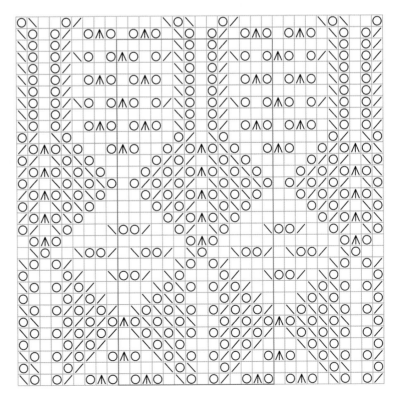

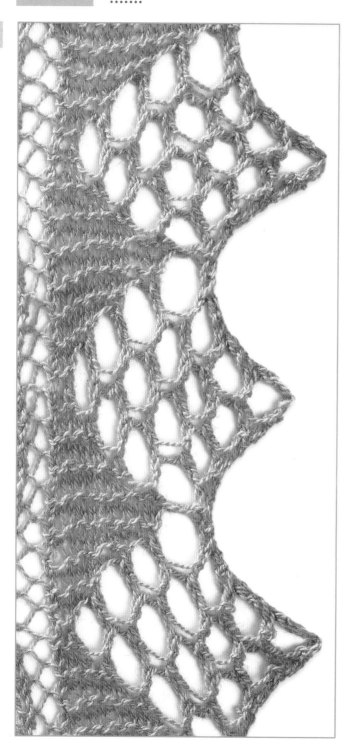

Drops Lace
▶ LACE

An old lace, ideal to pair with designs using ot
lace hole patterns. Note that the ladder inserti
is part of this lace.

METHOD

Row 1: k10, k2tog, yo, k3
Row 2: k1, k2tog, yo, k11, kfb
Row 3: kfb, k2tog, yo, yo, ssk, k6, k2tog, yo, k3
Row 4: k1, k2tog, yo, k10, p1, k2, kfb
Row 5: kfb, [k2tog, yo, yo, ssk] twice, k4, k2tog, yo, k3
Row 6: k1, k2tog, yo, k8, p1, k3, p1, k2, kfb
Row 7: kfb, [k2tog, yo, yo, ssk] three times, k2, k2tog, yo, k3
Row 8: k1, k2tog, yo, k6, [p1, k3] three times
Row 9: [k2tog, yo, yo, ssk] four times, k2tog, yo,
Row 10: k1, k2tog, yo, k4, [p1, k3] three times, p1,
Row 11: ssk, [k2tog, yo, yo, ssk] three times, k2, k2tog, yo, k3
Row 12: k1, k2tog, yo, k6, [p1, k3] twice, p1, k2tog
Row 13: ssk, [k2tog, yo, yo, ssk] twice, k4, k2tog, yo, k3
Row 14: k1, k2tog, yo, k8, p1, k3, p1, k2tog
Row 15: ssk, k2tog, yo, yo, ssk, k6, k2tog, yo, k3
Row 16: k1, k2tog, yo, k10, p1, k2tog

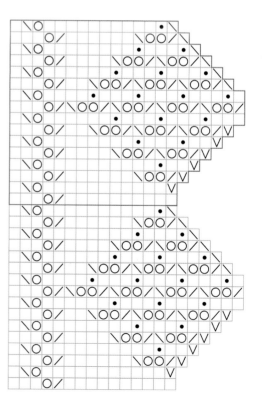

Victorian Zigzag Lace

▶ LACE

Another old lace used in many Shetland items. If you look at the pattern you can see it could be broken down into a steek, the zigzag insertion and the edging with the lace holes. The zigzags could be used separately.

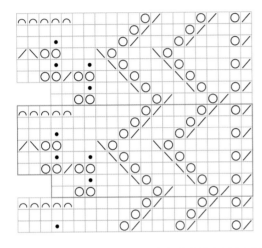

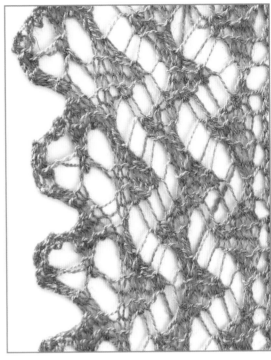

shown at 75%

Lace Holes

▶ MOTIF*

This simple little motif is used in many ways. The double yo gives a big hole which will stretch in the direction required. Note that on the second row, the second yo is usually PURLED. This makes a neater hole. If you find your hole is too big with the two yos, just do one—but remember to knit and purl into that one yo in the return row.

*Also features as insertion page 54, insertion page 66, lace page 110

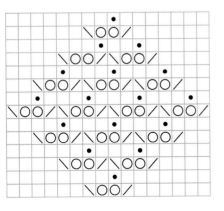

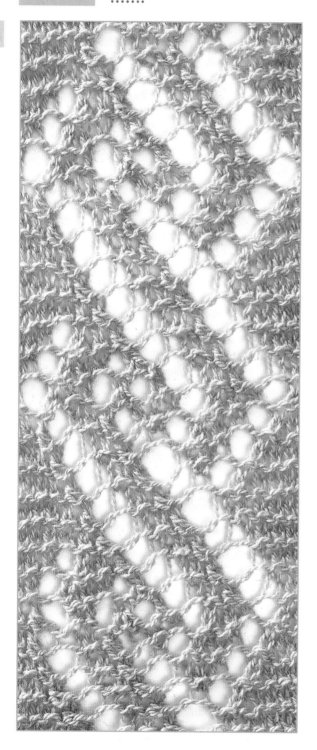

Lace Cable
▸ **MOTIF**

This motif can be used as charted or as a "stripe" between other motifs. It needs several plain stitches on each side for the effect of the "cable" to show.

METHOD

Row 1: k5, [yo, ssk, k2] twice, k3
Row 2 and all alternate rows: k
Row 3: k3, k2tog, yo, k1, [yo, ssk, k2] twice, k2
Row 5: k2, k2tog, yo, k3, [yo, ssk, k2] twice, k1
Row 7: k1, k2tog, yo, k2, k2tog, yo, k1, [yo, ssk, k2] twice
Row 9: k2tog, yo, k2, k2tog, yo, k3, yo, ssk, k2, yo, ssk, k1
Row 11: [k2, yo, ssk] twice, yo, k3togtbl, yo, k2, k2tog, yo, k1
Row 13: k3, yo, ssk, k2, yo, k3togtbl, yo, k2, k2tog, yo, k2
Row 15: k2, [k2, yo, ssk] twice, k1, k2tog, yo, k3
Row 16: k

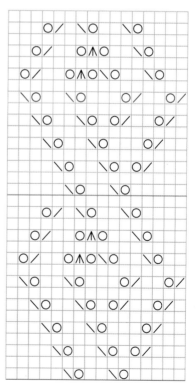

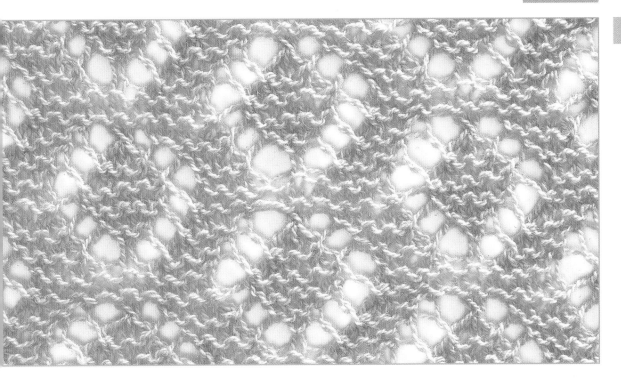

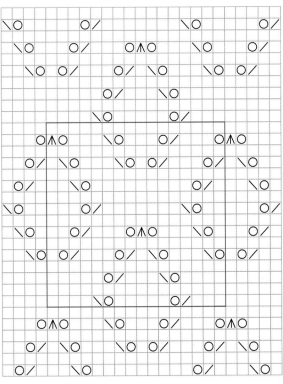

Mrs Montague's Pattern

▶ **ALL-OVER**

An old shawl center. It works well for baby blankets in thicker yarns too.

METHOD

Row 1: *k5, yo, ssk, k3, k2tog, yo, k4. Repeat from * to last st, k1

Row 2 and all alternate rows: k

Row 3: *k1, yo, ssk, k3, yo, ssk, k1, k2tog, yo, k3, k2tog, yo. Repeat from * to last st, k1

Row 5: *k2, yo, ssk, k3, yo, k3togtbl, yo, k3, k2tog, yo, k1. Repeat from * to last st, k1

Row 7: *k3, yo, ssk, k7, k2tog, yo, k2. Repeat from * to last st, k1

Row 9: *k2, k2tog, yo, k9, yo, ssk, k1. Repeat from * to last st, k1

Row 11: *k1, k2tog, yo, k3, k2tog, yo, k1, yo, ssk, k3, yo, ssk. Repeat from * to last st, k1

Row 13: k2tog, yo, *k3, k2tog, yo, k3, yo, ssk, k3, yo, k3togtbl, yo. Repeat from * to last 15 sts, k3, k2tog, yo, k3, yo, ssk, k3, yo, ssk

Row 15: *k4, k2tog, yo, k5, yo, ssk, k3. Repeat from * to last st, k1

Row 16: k

STITCH DIRECTORY

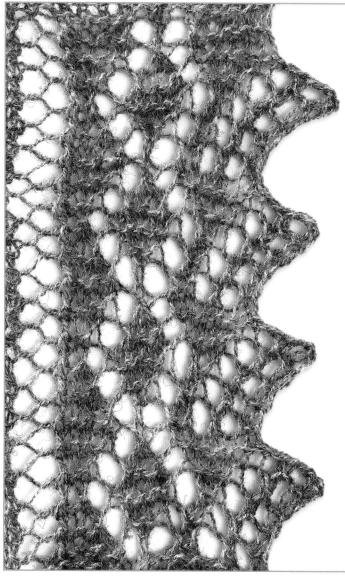

shown at 85%

Traditional Peaked Lac

▸ **LACE**

Used on thousands of hap and other shaw
over the years, this lace is still very versatile
The ladder insertion is part of the old lace.

METHOD

Rows 1, 3, 5, 7: s1p, k to last 3 sts, yo, ssk

Row 2: k2, yo, ssk, k1, k2tog, yo, k3, yo, ssk, k
yo, ssk, yo, k2

Row 4: k2, yo, ssk, k2tog, yo, k5, yo, ssk, k1, y
ssk, yo, k2

Row 6: k2, yo, ssk, k2, yo, ssk, k1, k2tog, yo, k
yo, ssk, yo, k2

Row 8: k2, yo, ssk, k3, yo, k3togtbl, yo, k6, y
ssk, yo, k2

Row 9: bind off 5, k to last 3 sts, yo, ssk

Row 10: k2, yo, ssk, k2, k2tog, yo, [k1, yo,
k2tog] twice, yo, k2

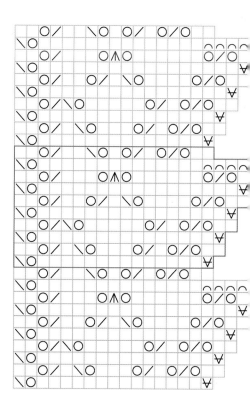

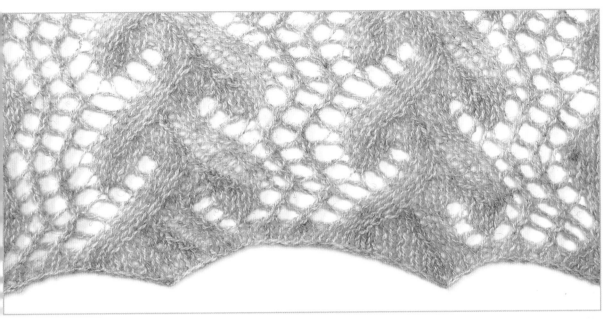

shown at 75%

Print of the Wave

▶ ALL-OVER

This well-known pattern is one of the few which needs to be worked on a STOCKINETTE-STITCH background for all but the finest yarns. This means that the even-numbered rows are PURL not knit. Although the actions are easy, it needs quite a bit of concentration as the yos and the decreases are removed from each other in different ways on different rows.

METHOD

Row 1: k2, [k2tog, yo] twice, *k2tog, yo, k1, yo, k2, ssk, k4, k2tog, k2, yo, k2tog, yo. Repeat from * to last 4 sts, k2tog, yo, k2

Row 2 and all alternate rows: p

Row 3: k1, [k2tog, yo] twice, k2tog, *yo, k3, yo, k2, ssk, k2, k2tog, k2, [yo, k2tog] twice. Repeat from * to last 3 sts, yo, k3

Row 5: [k2tog, yo] three times, *k5, yo, k2, ssk, k2tog, k2, [yo, k2tog] twice, yo. Repeat from * to last 4 sts, k4

Row 7: k2, [yo, ssk] twice, *yo, k2, ssk, k4, k2tog, k2, yo, k1, [yo, ssk] twice. Repeat from * to last 4 sts, yo, ssk, k2

Row 9: k3, yo, ssk, yo, *ssk, yo, k2, ssk, k2, k2tog, k2, yo, k3, yo, ssk, yo. Repeat from * to last 5 sts, ssk, yo, ssk, k1

Row 11: k4, yo, ssk, *yo, ssk, yo, k2, ssk, k2tog, k2, yo, k5, yo, ssk. Repeat from * to last 4 sts, [yo, ssk] twice

Row 12: p

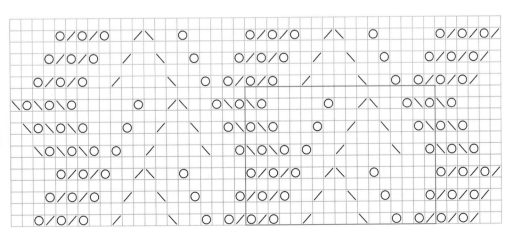

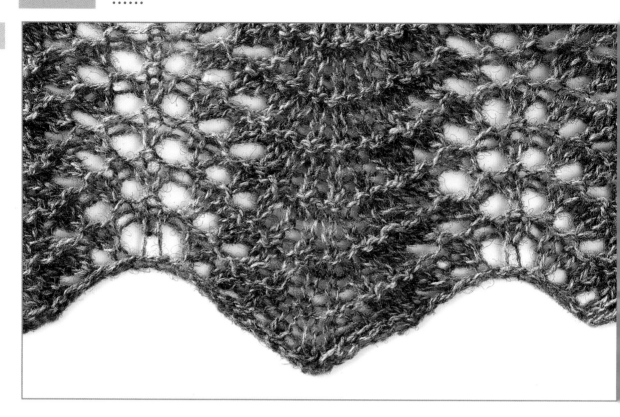

Old Shale

▶ **ALL-OVER**

This pattern was the traditional border for the hap shawls worn by every woman in the Northern Isles. In Shetland it is called Old Shell—"shale" was a mistake by early pattern collectors, caused by the Shetland accent, but it has stuck! Note that it is worked on a stockinette-stitch background.

METHOD

Row 1: *k2tog three times, [yo, k1] six times, k2tog three times. Repeat from * to end of row.

Rows 2 and 3: k

Row 4: p

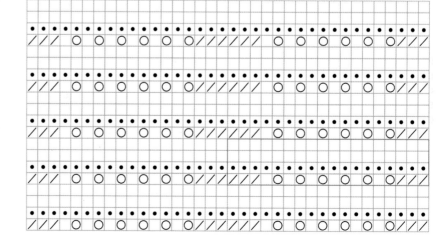

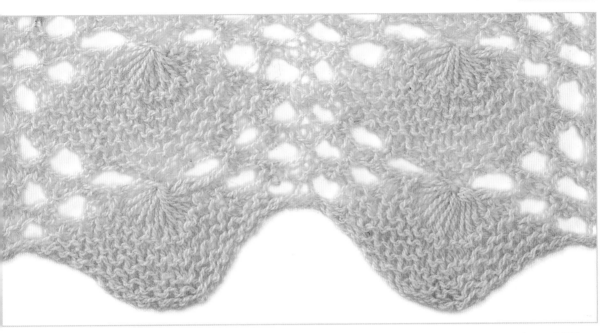

shown at 85%

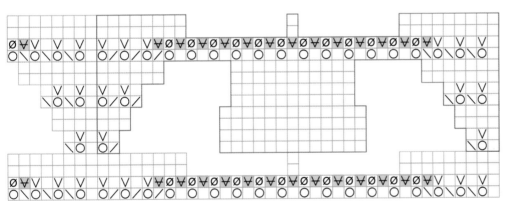

Cockleshell

▶ ALL-OVER

This pattern is used almost exclusively for scarves, but it would also make a pretty shawl border. Make sure you cast on very loosely so that the scallops can form. Note that the stitch count changes on different rows.

METHOD

Row 1: *k1, yo, ssk, k13, k2tog, yo. Repeat from * to last st, k1 (18 sts in repeat)

Row 2: *k1, k and p into the next st, k15, k and p into the next st. Repeat from * to last st, k1 (20 sts in repeat)

Rows 3 and 4: k

Row 5: *k1, [yo, ssk] twice, k11, [k2tog, yo] twice. Repeat from * to last st, k1

Row 6: *[k1, k and p into the next st] twice, k12, [k1, k and p into the next st] twice (24 sts in repeat)

Rows 7 and 8: k

Row 9: *k1, [yo, ssk] three times, [yo, k1] 11 times, yo, [k2tog, yo] three times. Repeat from * to last st, k1 (36 sts in repeat)

Row 10: *[k1, k and p into the next st] three times, [s1p, drop the yo] 12 times, s1p. Put the 13 slipped sts back onto the other needle and knit them together tbl, [k and p into the next st, k1] twice, k and p into the next st. Repeat from * to last st, k1 (18 sts in repeat)

Rows 11 and 12: k

18.20

Level 3
●●●●●●

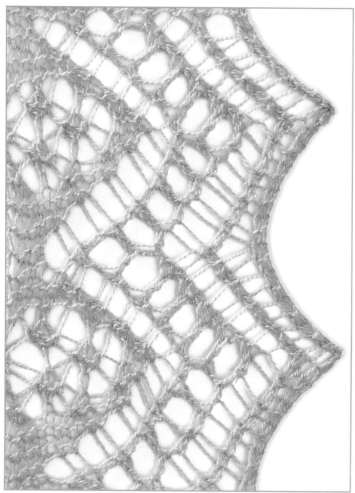

shown at 70%

Bead and Lace Holes

▶ **LACE***

This is a typical composite lace made up of simple zigzags, lace hole zigzags, and a bead cluster motif. For a wider lace add more simple zigzags or a ladder insertion.

*Bead also features as all-over page 59, insertion page 63, motif page 95
Lace Holes also features as insertion page 54, inserion page 66, motif page 103

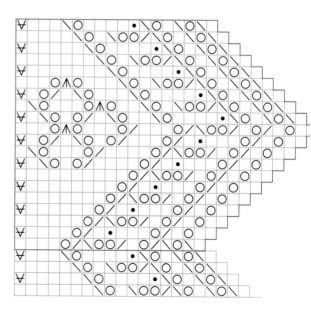

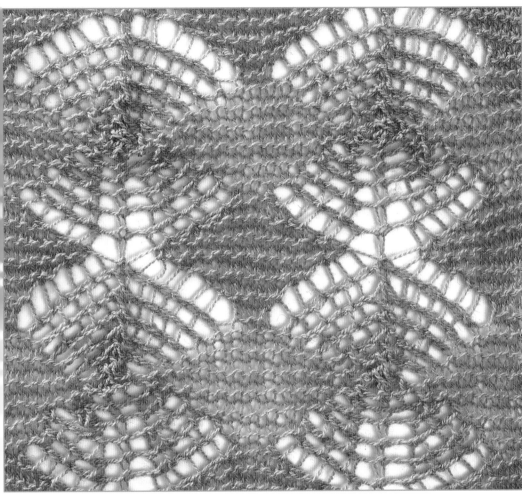

shown at 70%

Spider's Web
▶ **ALL-OVER**

This is one pattern where the chart looks very different from the knitted piece. Once knitted, the spines of decreases fold round to form the web. If another lacy pattern such as Lace Holes (page 54) or Fancy Net (page 74) is placed in the plain diamonds the effect is of a web of lace.

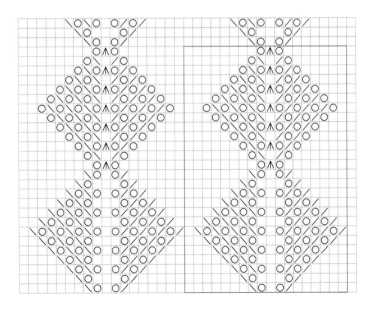

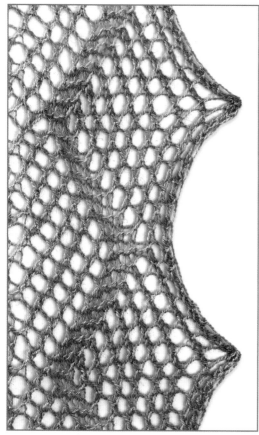

shown at 50%

Traditional Large Scalloped Lace

▶ **LACE**

This old, wide lace gives sweeping scallops rather than points, and can look lovely on a simple shawl.

METHOD

Row 1 and all alternate rows: yo, ssk, k to end of row
Row 2: s1p, k1, [yo, ssk] five times, k3, yo, ssk, yo, k2
Row 4: s1p, k2, [yo, ssk] four times, k3, [yo, ssk] twice, yo, k2
Row 6: s1p, k1, [yo, ssk] four times, k3, [yo, ssk] three times, yo, k2
Row 8: s1p, k2, [yo, ssk] three times, k3, [yo, ssk] four times, yo, k2
Row 10: s1p, k1, [yo, ssk] three times, k3, [yo, ssk] five times, yo, k2
Row 12: s1p, k2, [yo, ssk] twice, k3, [yo, ssk] six times, yo, k2
Row 14: s1p, k1, [yo, ssk] twice, k3, [yo, ssk] seven times, yo, k2
Row 16: s1p, k2, [yo, ssk] twice, k2, [k2tog, yo] seven times, k2tog, k1
Row 18: s1p, k1, [yo, ssk] three times, k2, [k2tog, yo] six times, k2tog, k1
Row 20: s1p, k2, [yo, ssk] three times, k2, [k2tog, yo] five times, k2tog, k1
Row 22: s1p, k1, [yo, ssk] four times, k2, [k2tog, yo] four times, k2tog, k1
Row 24: s1p, k2, [yo, ssk] four times, k2, [k2tog, yo] three times, k2tog, k1
Row 26: s1p, k1, [yo, ssk] five times, k2, [k2tog, yo] twice, k2tog, k1
Row 28: s1p, k2, [yo, ssk] five times, k2, k2tog, yo, k2tog, k1

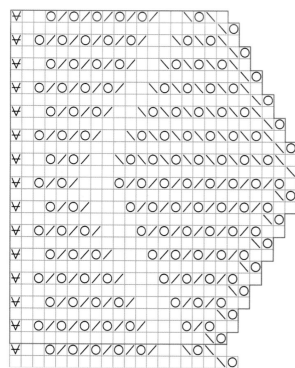

Irish, or Elaine, Lace

▶ **LACE**

Another old lace, this time with a very large hole as the focus. If you find your hole is too large, do two yos instead of three, then knit and purl into the first on the return row. Note that alternate rows start with the "yo, ssk" edge.

METHOD

Row 1: s1p, k1, [yo, ssk] four times, k3, k2tog, yo, k3, yo, k2

Rows 2, 4, 8, 10: yo, ssk, k to end of row

Row 3: s1p, k2, [yo, ssk] three times, k3, k2tog, yo, k5, yo, k2

Row 5: s1p, k1, [yo, ssk] three times, k3, k2tog, yo, ssk, k2tog, [yo] three times, ssk, k1, yo, k2

Row 6: yo, ssk, k4, p1, k to end of row

Row 7: s1p, k2, [yo, ssk] three times, k4, yo, ssk, k3, k2tog, yo, k2tog, k1

Row 9: s1p, k1, [yo, ssk] four times, k4, yo, ssk, k1, k2tog, yo, k2tog, k1

Row 11: s1p, k2, [yo, ssk] four times, k4, yo, k3togtbl, yo, k2tog, k1

Row 12: yo, ssk, k to end of row

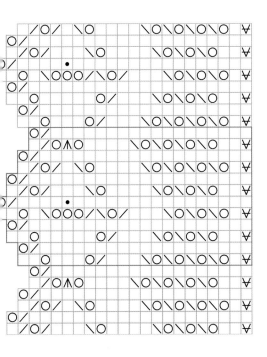

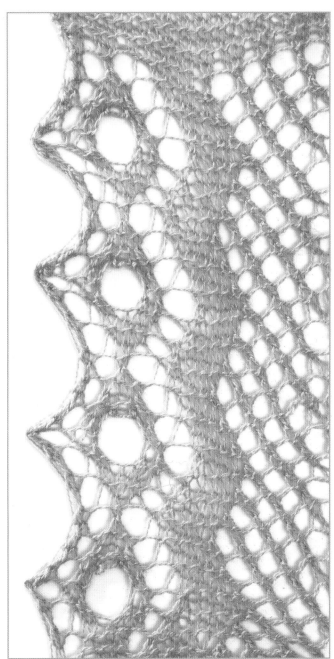

shown at 70%

20.20   Level 2
•••••••

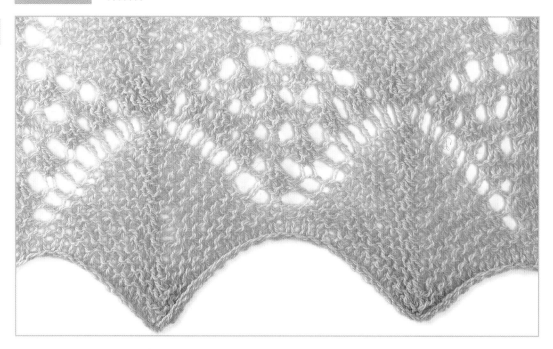

Madeira Cascade
▶ ALL-OVER

shown at 75%

A very old pattern which may have Spanish origins, or be a copy from Spanish lace. Note that this looks nothing like The Madeira (page 84).

METHOD

Row 1: *k1, yo, k8, k3togtbl, k8, yo. Repeat from * to last st, k1

Row 2 and all alternate rows: k

Row 3: *k2, yo, k7, k3togtbl, k7, yo, k1. Repeat from * to last st, k1

Row 5: k2tog, yo, *k1, yo, k6, k3togtbl, k6, yo, k1, yo, k3tog, yo. Repeat from * to last 19 sts, k1, yo, k6, k3togtbl, k6, yo, k1, yo, ssk

Row 7: *k4, yo, k5, k3togtbl, k5, yo, k3. Repeat from * to last st, k1

Row 9: *k1, yo, k3togtbl, yo, k4, k3togtbl, k4, yo, k1, yo, k3togtbl, yo. Repeat from * to last st, k1

Row 11: *k6, yo, k3, k3togtbl, k3, yo, k3. Repeat from * to last st, k1

Row 13: k2tog, yo, *k1, yo, k3togtbl, yo, k1, yo, k2, k3togtbl, k2, yo, [k1, yo, k3togtbl, yo] twice. Repeat from * to last 19 sts, k1, yo, k3togtbl, yo, k1, yo, k2, k3togtbl, k2, yo, k1, yo, k3togtbl, yo, k1, yo, ssk

Row 15: *k8, yo, k1, k3togtbl, k1, yo, k5. Repeat from * to last st, k1

Row 17: *k1, yo, k3togtbl, yo. Repeat from * to last st, k1

Rows 19 and 20: k

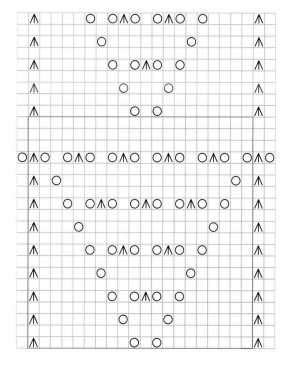

shown at 70%

Rose Diamond Frame with Rose Clusters

▶ ALL-OVER

The diamond frame has a rose at the intersections of the lines. The rose cluster motif is placed within the diamonds. The frame could be used with other motifs.

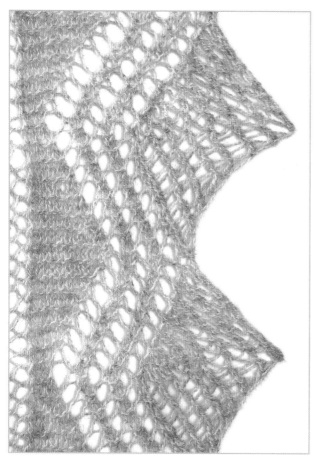

shown at 50%

Fan Lace

▶ **LACE**

This chart looks complex but once started it is easy to follow. Note that the even-numbered rows start with a yo. This lace can easily be made longer or shorter by adding or omitting rows in the middle of the chart.

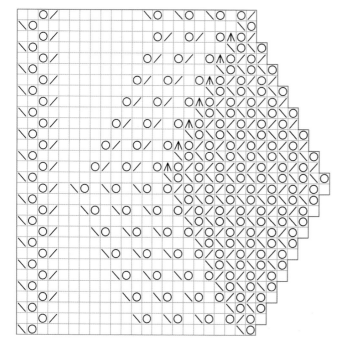

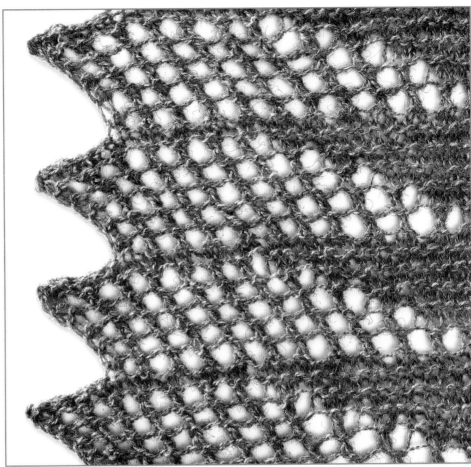

shown at 75%

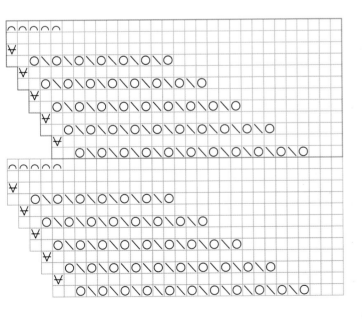

Margaret's Lace
▶ LACE

This is a version of a lace by Margaret Peterson of Unst. Its simplicity, and the plain areas sweeping to the points, make it ideal as a lace for simple shawls.

METHOD
Row 1: k3, [yo, ssk] ten times, yo, k2
Row 2 and all alternate rows: s1p, k to end
Row 3: k6, [yo, ssk] nine times, yo, k2
Row 5: k9, [yo, ssk] eight times, yo, k2
Row 7: k12, [yo, ssk] seven times, yo, k2
Row 9: k15, [yo, ssk] six times, yo, k2
Row 11: k
Row 12: bind off 5, k to end of row

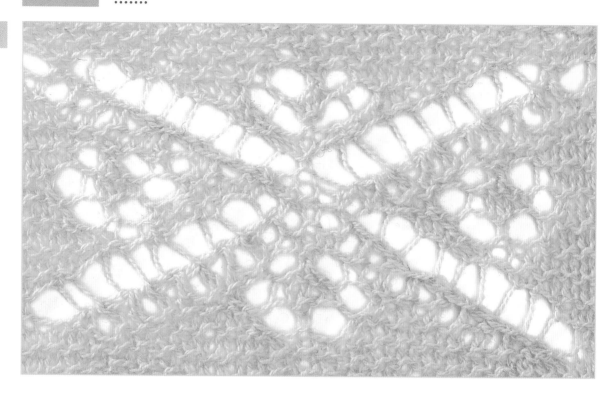

The Saltire

▶ **MOTIF**

The Scottish flag is the Cross of St Andrew, known in Scotland as the Saltire. It was used a lot in Shetland lace in the nineteenth and early twentieth centuries. Often, as here, a small motif was placed between the arms. I have used cat's paws, but you could exchange them for your favorite small motif.

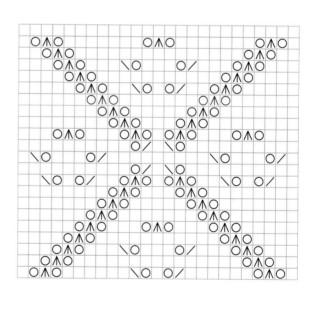

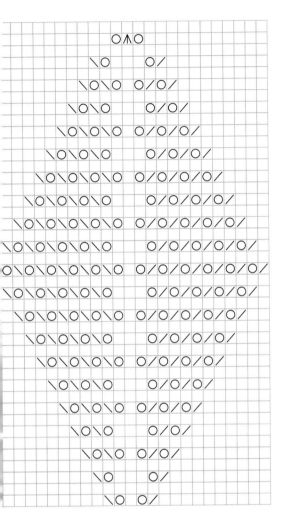

shown at 70%

Tree
▶ MOTIF

Trees can be made any size. They are often used on shawl borders.

METHOD

Row 1: k10, k2tog, yo, k1, yo, ssk, k10

Row 2 and all alternate rows: k

Row 3: k9, k2tog, yo, k3, yo, ssk, k9

Row 5: k8, [k2tog, yo] twice, k1, [yo, ssk] twice, k8

Row 7: k7, [k2tog, yo] twice, k3, [yo, ssk] twice, k7

Row 9: k6, [k2tog, yo] three times, k1, [yo, ssk] three times, k6

Row 11: k5, [k2tog, yo] three times, k3, [yo, ssk] three times, k5

Row 13: k4, [k2tog, yo] four times, k1, [yo, ssk] four times, k4

Row 15: k3, [k2tog, yo] four times, k3, [yo, ssk] four times, k3

Row 17: k2, [k2tog, yo] five times, k1, [yo, ssk] five times, k2

Row 19: k1, [k2tog, yo] five times, k3, [yo, ssk] five times, k1

Row 21: [k2tog, yo] six times, k1, [yo, ssk] six times

Row 23: as row 19

Row 25: as row 17

Row 27: as row 15

Row 29: as row 13

Row 31: as row 11

Row 33: as row 9

Row 35: as row 7

Row 37: as row 5

Row 39: as row 3

Row 41: k11, yo, k3togtbl, yo, k11

Row 42: k

PROJECTS

The stitches in this book can be combined and used in a myriad of ways. This chapter presents a selection of stunning designs to inspire you with ideas of how to use the stitches in your own projects.

LEFT Shoulder Shawl, pages 129–131
ABOVE Crescent Shawl, pages 140–141

FAR LEFT Hat and Scarf set,
(hat not shown),
pages 126–128
LEFT Cobweb Shawl,
pages 124–125

TOP Baby Set, including
jacket (shown), mittens
and bonnet (not shown),
pages 132–135
CENTER Lacy Mitts,
pages 136–137
BOTTOM Ten-stitch Socks,
pages 138–139

MATERIALS
- 600yd (550m): 1¼oz (35g) 1 ply yarn
- A pair of size 2 (3mm) knitting needles
- Row counter
- Waste yarn

SIZE
Approximately 25½in (65cm) square

GAUGE
Approximately 20 sts and 44 rows to 4in (10cm) over the center pattern. The shawl is very stretchy.

ALTERNATIVE STITCHES YOU CAN USE:

Central cluster:

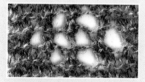

Fancy Net, page 74

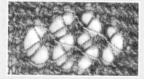

Bead Cluster, page 95

Lace:

Bead Insertion, page 63   Victorian Zigzag Lace, page 103

Cobweb Shawl

Light as a feather but surprisingly warm, this small shawl is both pretty and practical. Made from cobweb yarn, it is fine enough to fit through a wedding ring. There are yos only on odd numbered rows, so it isn't difficult to knit.

Lace
With waste yarn, cast on 11 sts. Change to main yarn and work through the eight rows of the Lace Chart 108 times. Leave sts on a thread for grafting later.

Center
With one needle and RS facing, starting at the cast-on end, pick up a total of 216 sts from the straight edge of the lace, one for every s1p. Now with the other needle and WS facing, starting at the end with the sts on the holder, pick up a total of 216 sts from the straight edge of the lace, one for every s1p. The needle tips should face each other in the center of the lace strip. With RS facing, rejoin yarn here, and work TO AND FRO as follows:

Row 1 (RS): s1p, k103, ssk, turn
Row 2: as row 1

Now work from the Center Chart over these 105 sts, working the 20 st repeat four times per row, and decreasing at the end of every row as shown. Work through the 44 rows of the chart a total of five times.
Next Row: s1p, k to end of row.

Finishing
Graft remaining stitches from the center to the picked-up sts along final length of lace. Remove the waste yarn from the start of the lace and graft these stitches to the live stitches at the end of the lace. Weave in all ends. Wash and dress the shawl, and when dry, cut off all ends.

Center Chart

Lace Chart

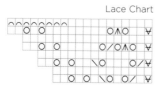

PROJECTS

MATERIALS
- 410yd (375m): 5¼oz (150g) Aran weight yarn
- A pair of size 11 (8mm) knitting needles
- Row counter
- Tapestry needle

SIZE
Scarf 12in (30cm) wide and 60in (152cm) long. The length is easily adjustable. The hat is very stretchy and will fit teens and adults with a head circumference of up to 23in (59cm).

GAUGE
12 sts and 24 rows to 4in (10cm) in garter stitch.

ALTERNATIVE STITCHES YOU CAN USE:
Instead of Cat's Paw, try:

Spider Motif, page 64

Bead Insertion, page 63   Eyelid Insertion, page 65

Strawberry, page 71

Hat and Scarf Set

A warm set that knits up quickly. The scarf is made using Cat's Paw lace with three insertions. Why not use your own motifs?

Scarf

Cast on 33 sts and knit 1 row. Work through the twenty-four rows of the Scarf Chart ten times or to desired length, finishing after row 12. Bind off.

Scarf Chart
Row 1: s1p, k1, yo, k2tog, yo, k5, yo, k3togtbl, yo, k2, k2tog, yo, k1, yo, ssk, k2, yo, k3togtbl, yo, k5, yo, ssk, yo, k2

Row 2 and all alternate rows: s1p, k to end of row

Row 3: s1p, k1, yo, k2tog, yo, k6, yo, k3togtbl, yo, k1, k2tog, yo, k3, yo, ssk, k1, yo, k3togtbl, yo, k6, yo, ssk, yo, k2

Row 5: s1p, k1, yo, k2tog, yo, k7, [yo, k3togtbl, yo, k3] twice, yo, k3togtbl, yo, k7, yo, ssk, yo, k2

Row 7: s1p, k1, yo, k2tog, yo, k8, yo, k3togtbl, yo, k9, yo, k3togtbl, yo, k8, yo, ssk, yo, k2

Row 9: s1p, k1, yo, k2tog, [yo, k2, k2tog, yo, k1, yo, ssk, k2, yo, k3togtbl] twice, yo, k2, k2tog, yo, k1, yo, ssk, k2, yo, ssk, yo, k2

Row 11: s1p, k1, yo, k2tog, yo, k2, [k2tog, yo, k3, yo, ssk, k1, yo, k3togtbl, yo, k1] twice, k2tog, yo, k3, yo, ssk, k2, yo, ssk, yo, k2

Row 13: s1p, [ssk, yo] twice, ssk, k2, [yo, k3togtbl, yo, k3] four times, yo, k3togtbl, yo, k2, [k2tog, yo] twice, k2tog, k1

Row 15: s1p, [ssk, yo] twice, ssk, k7, yo, k3togtbl, yo, k9, yo, k3togtbl, yo, k7, [k2tog, yo] twice, k2tog, k1

Row 17: s1p, [ssk, yo] twice, ssk, k6, yo, k3togtbl, yo, k2, k2tog, yo, k1, yo, ssk, k2, yo, k3togtbl, yo, k6, [k2tog, yo] twice, k2tog, k1

Row 19: s1p, [ssk, yo] twice, ssk, k5, yo, k3togtbl, yo, k1, k2tog, yo, k3, yo, ssk, k1, yo, k3togtbl, yo, k5, [k2tog, yo] twice, k2tog, k1

Row 21: s1p, [ssk, yo] twice, ssk, k4, [yo, k3togtbl, yo, k3] twice, yo, k3togtbl, yo, k4, [k2tog, yo] twice, k2tog, k1

Row 23: s1p, [ssk, yo] twice, ssk, k3, yo, k3togtbl, yo, k9, yo, k3togtbl, yo, k3, [k2tog, yo] twice, k2tog, k1

Row 24: as row 2

Scarf Chart

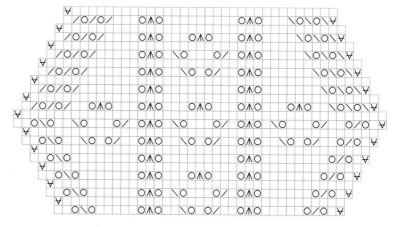

Hat

Cast on 9 sts and knit 1 row. Work through the twenty-four rows of the Hat Chart four times. Bind off. For the crown, pick up 48 sts from the straight edge of the brim [1 for every s1p]. Knit 24 rows. Shape top as follows:

Row 1: *k6, k2tog. Repeat from * to end of row

Rows 2, 4, 6, 8: k

Row 3: *k5, k2tog. Repeat from * to end of row

Row 5: *k4, k2tog. Repeat from * to end of row

Row 7: *k3, k2tog. Repeat from * to end of row

Row 9: *k2, k2tog. Repeat from * to end of row

Row 10: *k1, k2tog. Repeat from * to end of row

Row 11: k2tog along row. Break yarn and draw through 6 remaining sts.

Hat Chart

Row 1: s1p, k4, yo, ssk, yo, k2

Row 2 and all alternate rows: s1p, k to end of row

Row 3: s1p, k5, yo, ssk, yo, k2

Row 5: s1p, k6, yo, ssk, yo, k2

Row 7: s1p, k7, yo, ssk, yo, k2

Row 9: s1p, k1, k2tog, yo, k1, yo, ssk, k2, yo, ssk, yo, k2

Row 11: s1p, k2tog, yo, k3, yo, ssk, k2, yo, ssk, yo, k2

Row 13: s1p, k2, yo, k3togtbl, yo, k2, [k2tog, yo] twice, k2tog, k1

Row 15: s1p, k6, [k2tog, yo] twice, k2tog, k1

Row 17: s1p, k5, [k2tog, yo] twice, k2tog, k1

Row 19: s1p, k4, [k2tog, yo] twice, k2tog, k1

Row 21: s1p, k3, [k2tog, yo] twice, k2tog, k1

Row 23: s1p, k2, [k2tog, yo] twice, k2tog, k1

Row 24: s1p, k to end of row

Finishing

Sew up hat seam, reversing the seam for the brim. Weave in ends. Wash and dry hat and scarf flat, pulling the scallop points to shape. Fold hat brim up to wear.

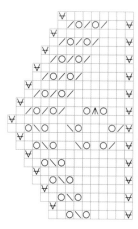

ATERIALS

00yd (550m): 5¼oz (150g)
arn A plus 40yd (37m):
⅜oz (10g) each Yarn B
nd C; all 4 ply
A pair of size 10 (6mm)
nitting needles
2in (80cm) circular needle
ize 10 (6mm)
ow counter
stitch markers
Vaste yarn
apestry needle

ZE

proximately 33in
5cm) square

AUGE

proximately 12 sts and
rows to 4in (10cm) over
e center pattern. The shawl
very stretchy.

**LTERNATIVE STITCHES
OU CAN USE:**

enter:

Shoulder Shawl

This is a modern version of the old hap shawls, worn by all women in the Northern Isles for generations. It is ideal to throw over your shoulders when the temperature drops

t's Eye, page 55

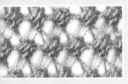

ncy Net, page 56

rd's Eye, page 59

ace:

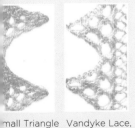

mall Triangle   Vandyke Lace,
ace, page 58   page 61

Center

With straight needles and waste yarn, cast on 59 sts. Change to Yarn A and work as follows:

Edging Row: s1p, k to end of row Repeat the edging row three times more. Work through the twelve rows of the Center Chart nine times, then work the edging row four times. Do not break yarn.

Center Chart

Row 1: s1p, *k2tog, yo, k4. Repeat from * to last 4 sts, k2tog, yo, k2

Row 2 and all alternate rows: s1p, k to end of row

Row 3: s1p, k1, *k1, yo, ssk, k1, k2tog, yo. Repeat from * to last 3 sts, k3

Row 5: s1p, *k3, yo, k3togtbl, yo. Repeat from * to last 4 sts, k4

Row 7: s1p, *k3, k2tog, yo, k1. Repeat from * to last 4 sts, k4

Row 9: s1p, k1, *k1, k2tog, yo, k1, yo, ssk. Repeat from * to last 3 sts, k3

Row 11: s1p, k1, k2tog, yo,*k3, yo, k3togtbl, yo. Repeat from * to last 7 sts, k3, yo, ssk, k2

Row 12: s1p, k to end of row

Border

With the same yarn and the circular needle, work as follows:

Round 1: k59, PM, pick up and k59 sts to waste yarn at cast-on edge (1 st in each s1p of the row ends of the center), PM, remove the waste yarn at the start of the center and k these 59 sts, PM, pick up and k59 sts along the side of the center, PM. Join and work in the round.

Round 2: *p29, m1, k to next M, SM. Repeat from * to end of round. Four sets of 60 sts

Round 3: *[yo, kfb] three times, [yo, k2tog] to 3 sts before next M, [yo, kfb] three times, SM. Repeat from * to end of round. Four sets of 72 sts

Round 4: p

Change to Yarn B and start the Old Shale pattern as follows:

Round 1: *[yo, k1] three times, k2tog six times, [yo, k1] three times. Repeat from * to end of round

Round 2: p

Rounds 3 and 4: k

Repeat these 4 rounds in Yarn A, then Yarn C, then Yarn A, then Yarn B, then Yarn A, then Yarn C. Finish with rounds 1 to 3 in Yarn A. Do not break yarn.

Center Chart

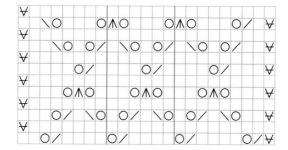

Lace

With waste yarn and the straight needles, cast on 9 sts and knit 1 row. With the Yarn A from the border, work the Lace Chart across these sts, noting that for every twelve row repeat, 6 stitches are removed from the border (1 at the end of each alternate row). Once all the stitches have been removed, take out the waste yarn from the start of the lace and graft these two sets of live stitches together.

Lace Chart

Row 1: s1p, k2, [k2tog, yo] twice, k1, yo, k1

Row 2: s1p, k8, knb

Row 3: s1p, k1, [k2tog, yo] twice, k3, yo, k1

Row 4: s1p, k9, knb

Row 5: s1p, [k2tog, yo] twice, k5, yo, k1

Row 6: s1p, k10, knb

Row 7: s1p, k2, [yo, ssk] twice, k1, k2tog, yo, k2tog

Row 8: s1p, k9, knb

Row 9: s1p, k3, yo, ssk, yo, k3togtbl, yo, k2tog

Row 10: s1p, k8, knb

Row 11: s1p, k4, yo, ssk, k1, k2tog

Row 12: s1p, k7, knb

Finishing

Weave in all ends. Wash and dress the shawl. When dry, cut off all ends.

Lace Chart

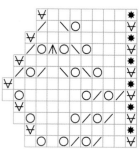

MATERIALS

- 500yd (460m): 3¹/₂oz (100g) 3 ply yarn
- A pair of size 4 (3.5mm) and a pair of size 7 (4.5mm) knitting needles
- Row counter
- Waste yarn
- Tapestry needle
- 2yd (2m) narrow ribbon if desired
- 3 small buttons about ³/₈in (9mm) in diameter for the jacket

SIZE

To fit about 3 to 9 months. The jacket has a chest of 18in (46cm) and is 11in (28cm) long with sleeves 5in (13cm) long.

The mittens are 5in (13cm) long and 6in (15cm) round.

The bonnet is 12in (30cm) round the face.

The set is very stretchy.

GAUGE

28 sts and 56 rows to 4in (10cm) in garter stitch, unstretched, on size 4 (3.5mm) needles. Pattern on size 3 (3mm) needles.

ALTERNATIVE STITCHES YOU CAN USE:

Instead of Spider, try:

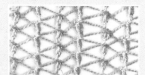

Fagotting, page 53

Bird's Eye, page 59

Flee Motif, page 62

Baby Set

Make this set in a machine-washable wool yarn: it will keep baby warm and be easy for mom to wash and dry. It is sure to get plenty of use (and compliments)!

Mittens

Cuff

With size 7 (4.5mm) needles, cast on 11 sts and k 1 row. Work through the eight rows of the Mitten Chart six times. Bind off.

Hand

With size 4 (3.5mm) needles and RS facing, pick up 24 sts from the straight edge of the cuff (1 st in every s1p).

Row 1 (RS): *k1, kfb, k1. Repeat from * to end of row. 32 sts

Row 2: k

Row 3: *k1, yo, ssk, k1. Repeat from * to end of row

Rows 4 to 30: k

Row 31: *k2, k2tog. Repeat from * to end of row

Row 32: k

Row 33: *k1, k2tog. Repeat from * to end of row

Row 34: k

Row 35: k2tog along row
Break yarn and draw through remaining sts.

Finishing

Sew side seam and weave in ends. Wash and dry flat, pinning out the peaks around the wrist. Make two yarn cords about 12in (30cm) long and thread through the holes in the Ladder Insertion, or use ribbon.

Mitten Chart

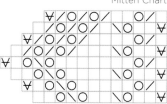

Bonnet

Brim

With size 7 (4.5mm) needles and waste yarn, cast on 24 sts. Change to the correct yarn and k 1 row. Work through the eight rows of the Hat and Sleeve Chart twelve times.

Next Row (RS): s1p, k2, yo, k3togtbl, yo, k to end of row
Place these 24 sts on a length of waste yarn.

Back

With size 4 (3.5mm) needles and RS of brim facing, pick up 49 sts from the straight edge of the brim (1 st in every s1p).

Join yarn and work across the sts as follows: k1, [k1, yo, k1] to end of row. 73 sts

Row 1: k1, *k2, k2tog, yo, k3togtbl, yo, ssk, k3. Repeat from * to end of row

Rows 2 to 4: s1p, k to end of row
Row 5: k1, *k1, k2tog, yo, k3togtbl, yo, ssk, k2. Repeat from * to end of row

Rows 6 to 8: s1p, k to end of row
Row 9: k1, *k2tog, yo, k3togtbl, yo, ssk, k1. Repeat from * to end of row

Rows 10 to 12: s1p, k to end of row

Row 13: k2tog, *yo, k3togtbl. Repeat from * to last 2 sts, ssk
Rows 14 to 16: s1p, k to end of row
Row 17: k1, *yo, k3togtbl. Repeat from * to last 2 sts, ssk
Rows 18 to 20: s1p, k to end of row
Row 21: k1, k3togtbl five times. Break yarn and draw up remaining 6 sts. Fold in half at center and sew back seam.

Neck Band

Remove waste yarn at the start of the brim. With RS facing, place these 24 sts on a size 4 (3.5mm) needle, pick up 1 st from the end of the back seam, and then add the 24 live sts from the other end of the brim. 49 sts
K 2 rows.
Next Row: s1p, *k1, yo, ssk, k1. Repeat from * to end of row
Next Row: s1p, k to end of row
Repeat these two rows twice more.
Bind off.

Finishing

Weave in ends. Wash and dry flat, pinning out the peaks round the face. Make a yarn cord about 30in (75cm) long and thread through the holes in the neckband, or use ribbon.

Hat and Sleeve Chart

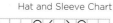

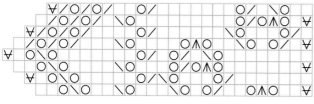

Jacket

Sleeves (2 alike)

With size 7 (4.5mm) needles and waste yarn cast on 24 sts. Change to the correct yarn and k 1 row. Work through the eight rows of the Hat and Sleeve Chart six times. Bind off.

Skirt

With size 7 (4.5mm) needles, cast on 34 sts and k 3 rows. Work through the eight rows of the Jacket Chart 24 times, then rows 1 to 5 again. K 3 rows. Bind off.

Yoke

With size 4 (3.5mm) needles and RS of the skirt facing, pick up the 98 loops from the straight edge of the skirt (1 st in every s1p). Work as follows:

Row 1 (RS): *k1, kfb, k3, kfb, k1. Repeat from * to end of row. 126 sts

Row 2: s1p, k to end of row

Row 3: s1p, k1, k2tog, yo, k to last 4 sts, yo, ssk, k2

Row 4: s1p, k3, yo, ssk, k to last 6 sts, k2tog, yo, k4

Row 5: s1p, k1, k2tog, yo, k29. Leave the next 60 sts on a thread for the Back and the remaining 33 sts on another thread for the Left Front. Turn

Row 6: k to last 6 sts, k2tog, yo, k4

Right Front

Row 1: s1p, k1, k2tog, yo, k to end of row

Row 2: k to last 6 sts, k2tog, yo, k4
Continue on these sts with a slipped stitch at the front edge but NOT at the armhole edge, until the armhole measures 2in (5cm) unstretched, ending after a WS row. Shape neck as follows:

Row 1 (RS): s1p, k11. Put these 12 sts on a thread for the neck band. K to end of row. 21 sts

Row 2: k

Row 3: k2tog, k to end of row

Row 4: k
Repeat rows 3 and 4 five times more. Bind off remaining 15 sts.

Back

Return to the 60 sts held for the Back. With RS facing, rejoin yarn and knit in garter stitch for 3in (8cm).

Next Row: Bind off 15 sts, k to last 15 sts, bind off 15 sts. Place remaining 30 sts on a thread for the neck band.

Left Front

Return to the remaining 33 sts. With RS facing, rejoin yarn and work across the sts as follows:

Row 1: k to last 4 sts, yo, ssk, k2

Row 2: s1p, k3, yo, ssk, k to end of row

Continue on these sts with a slipped stitch at the front edge but NOT at the armhole edge, until the armhole measures 2in (5cm) unstretched, ending after a wrong-side row.

Shape neck as follows:

Row 1 (RSF): k21. Put remaining 12 sts of row on a thread for the neck band.

Row 2: k

Row 3: k to last 2 sts, ssk

Row 4: k
Repeat rows 3 and 4 five times more. Bind off remaining 15 sts.

Neck Band

Sew shoulder seams. With size 4 (3.5mm) needles and RS facing, rejoin yarn to the Right Front neck. Knit 12 sts from the thread, pick up and knit 8 sts from the side neck, knit the 30 sts from the Back neck, pick up and knit 8 sts from the left-side neck, then knit the 12 sts from the Left Front neck. 70 sts
K 4 rows, slipping the first stitch of every row purlwise. Bind off.

Finishing

Sew sleeve seams, then sew sleeves into armholes. Weave in all ends. Sew buttons onto front yoke. Wash and dry flat, pinning out the scallops of the lace.

Jacket Chart

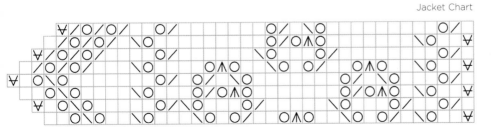

MATERIALS
- About 170yd (155m): ¹/₂oz (15g) lace weight yarn for each size
- A pair of size 3 (3mm), a pair of size 4 (3.5mm), and a pair of size 7 (4.5mm) knitting needles
- Row counter
- Tapestry needle
- 1yd (1m) narrow ribbon

SIZE
To fit a small/average/wide hand, palm circumference 5¹/₂in (14cm)/6¹/₂in (17cm)/7¹/₂in (19cm); hand length 3in (8cm)/4in (10cm)/5in (13cm). The mitts are very stretchy and the hand length can be easily altered.

GAUGE
28 sts and 32 rows to 4in (10cm) over the hand pattern on size 3 (3mm) needles

ALTERNATIVE STITCHES YOU CAN USE:
Cuffs:

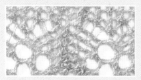

Da Puzzle, page 101

Hand:

Arches, page 63

Spider Motif, page 64

Lacy Mitts

These mitts are very simple to make yet look very elegant. They are an ideal first project in skinny yarn. Make them in white for a summer wedding, or black for a night at the opera!

Cuff
With size 7 (4.5mm) needles, cast on 57 sts loosely. Knit 1 row. Work through the four rows of the Cuff Chart a total of three/four/four times. Change to size 4 (3.5mm) needles and work through the chart three/three/four times more.
Make holes for the ribbon as follows: k1, *k1, yo, ssk, k1. Repeat from * to end of row. K 3 rows.

Cuff Chart
Row 1: *k1, k4tog, [yo, k1] five times, yo, k4togtbl. Repeat from * to last st, k1
Rows 2 to 4: k

Now decrease according to your size as follows:
Small hand: k2tog twice, *k2tog, k2. Repeat from * to last 5 sts, k2tog, k3. 42 sts
Average hand: *k5, k2tog. Repeat from * to last st, k1. 49 sts
Wide hand: k2tog, k to end of row. 56 sts

Hand
Change to size 3 (3mm) needles and work through the two rows of the Hand Chart thirteen/fifteen/seventeen times. Adjust hand length here. Knit 1 row. Bind off.

Hand Chart
Row 1: *k1, yo, k1, k3togtbl, k1, yo, k1. Repeat from * to end of row
Row 2: k

Make a second mitt the same.

Finishing
Fold the piece in half and sew down about 1in (2cm) from the top, leave a gap of about 1in (2cm) for the thumb, then sew the rest of the seam. Thread ribbon through the wrist.

Cuff Chart

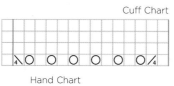

Hand Chart

MATERIALS

- 100yd (90m): ⁷/₈oz (25g)/150yd (140m): 1¹/₄oz (35g)/230yd (210m): 2oz (55g)/275yd (250m): 2¹/₄oz (65g) 4 ply sock yarn
- A set of size 2 (2.5mm)/ size 4 (3mm)/size 2 (2.5mm)/size 4 (3mm) double-pointed needles
- Row counter
- 2 stitch markers
- Tapestry needle

SIZE

To fit a toddler/child/ average adult/large adult foot. Foot length 4in (10cm)/5in (13cm)/7¹/₂in (19cm)/9in (23cm). Exact measurements will vary depending on gauge over chosen lace pattern. The leg and foot length can be easily altered.

GAUGE

32 sts and 44 rows on size 2 (2.5mm) needles, and 28 sts and 36 rows on size 4 (3.5mm) needles, to 4in (10cm) in stockinette stitch

ALTERNATIVE STITCHES YOU CAN USE:

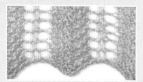

New Shell, page 75

Horse Shoe, page 76

Candle Light, page 79

Ten-stitch Socks

These basic socks can be made using any pattern with a 10 st repeat. Just be careful to note the start and end of the pattern after the heel.

Cuff

With the needle for your size, cast on 40/40/60/60 sts loosely. Join into a circle. P 1 round, then k 1 round.

Change to the pattern for the leg. Use any 10 st repeat pattern, such as Horse Shoe, New Shell or Candle Light, on a stockinette stitch background until the sock measures 3in (7cm)/4in (10cm)/ 6in (15cm)/7in (18cm) from cast on. Adjust leg length here.

Heel

Pattern 31/31/46/46. 9/9/14/14 sts remain. Place the first 10/10/15/15 sts worked onto the same needle as the remaining sts. These 19/19/ 29/29 sts are now worked as the heel, leaving the other 21/21/31/31 sts to be worked later for the top of the foot.

Row 1: k19/19/29/29 across the heel sts, turn

Row 2: p across heel sts

Work to and fro on these sts in stockinette stitch for 18/18/28/28 rows more.

Turn the heel

Row 1 (RS): k12/12/18/18, ssk, turn
Row 2: sl1, p5/5/7/7, p2tog, turn
Row 3: sl1, k5/5/7/7, ssk, turn
Row 4: sl1, p5/5/7/7, p2tog, turn
Repeat the last two rows four/ four/eight/eight times more. 7/7/9/9 sts remain on the heel needle

Instep

Round 1: knit across the 7/7/9/9 sts of the heel; pick up and knit 10/10/15/15 sts from the side of the heel flap, PM; pattern across the 21/21/31/31 sts of the top of the

foot, PM; pick up and knit 10/10/15/15 sts down the heel flap. Now work 4/4/5/5 sts from the heel to make the end of the following rounds in the middle of the sole. 48/48/70/70 sts

Round 2: k to 2 sts before M, k2tog, SM, pattern to next M, SM, ssk, k to end of round (2 sts decreased)

Round 3: k to M, SM, pattern to next M, SM, k to end of round Repeat round 3 no/no/one/one times more.

Repeat the last 2/2/3/3 rounds until 40/40/60/60 sts remain. Continue working the sole in stockinette stitch and the top of the foot in pattern until the sock measures 3¹/₂in (9cm)/4in (10cm)/ 6in (15cm)/7¹/₂in (19cm) from the point of the heel. Adjust foot length here.

Toes

Round 1: k

Round 2: *k to 2 sts before M, k2tog, SM, ssk. Repeat from * once more, k to end of round Repeat rounds 1 and 2 until 24/24/28/28 sts remain. Knit to first marker, then remove both markers.

Graft the foot sts to the sole sts. Weave in all ends securely.

Make a second sock to match.

MATERIALS

- 460yd (420m): 2$\frac{1}{2}$oz (70g) lace weight yarn
- A pair of size 6 (4mm) knitting needles
- Waste yarn
- Row counter
- Tapestry needle

SIZE

64in (162cm) wide and 16–18in (41–46cm) deep

GAUGE

16 sts and 28 rows to 4in (10cm) over the Fancy Net center

ALTERNATIVE STITCHES YOU CAN USE:

Center:

Cat's Eye, page 55

Mrs Hunter's Pattern, page 57

Border

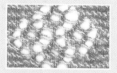

Rose Cluster, page 95

Lace Holes, page 105

Crescent Shawl

The shape of this shawl is very versatile. In summer drape it loosely over your arms for effect and in winter wrap it several times round your neck for warmth! The motifs in the border and lace are easily changed.

Center

Cast on 49 sts and knit 1 row. Work from the Center Chart until you have 185 sts on the needle. Put these sts on a thread.

Border

Pick up and knit 68 sts down one edge of the center (1 st for every row), pick up and knit 49 sts from the cast-on edge, then pick up and knit 68 sts from the other edge (1 st for every row). 185 sts

Row 1: s1p, k1, yo, k to last 2 sts, yo, k2

Repeat row 1 five times more. 197 sts

Work through the eight rows of the Border Chart once, then repeat row 1 (above) six times. 225 sts

Lace

With waste yarn cast on 12 sts and knit 1 row. Arrange these 12 sts for the Lace on one needle and the 225 Border stitches on the other. Change to the correct yarn and work from the thirty-two rows of the Lace Chart, removing sts from the Border as you go, until all the Border stitches have been removed. Knit one row to finish at the outer edge. Do not break the yarn.

Top Edge

Remove the waste yarn at the start of the Lace and place these 12 sts on a needle. On to the same needle, pick up 10 sts from the edge of the border, place the 185 sts from the top of the center on the needle, pick up 10 sts from the other border and finally place the live sts from the Lace.

Now k 4 rows across all sts. Bind off very loosely.

Finishing

Weave in all ends. Wash and dress, pinning out each point of the lace.

Lace Cha

Center Chart

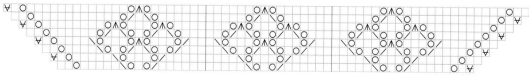

Border Chart

Index

A
Acre 48, 75
acrylic 16
all-overs 41
alpaca 16
Arches 48, 63

B
baby set 132–135
  bonnet 134
  jacket 135
  mittens 132
baby shawls 30
Bead and Lace Holes 50, 110
Bead Cluster 51, 95
Bead Insertion 50, 63
Bead Pattern 49, 59
binding off 19
Bird's Eye 48, 59
blocking mats 14
Brand Iron Lace 51, 90
Broken Acre 49, 78

C
Candle Light 49, 79
cashmere 16
casting on 18
Cat's Eye 48, 55
Cat's Paw 48, 77
Cat's Paw Insertion 50, 65
Cat's Paw Lace 50, 72
charting 36
  charting the edges 36
  charting the middle 36
  charting triangles 37
  making adjustments 37
charts 23
  reading a chart 23
  symbols 23
  symbols on even-numbered
    rows 23
  tips 23
Chevrons 49, 70
christening gowns 44
circles 32
  radial increases 33
  tiered increases 33
circular needles 14, 15
Coburg Lace 50, 86
Cockleshell 49, 109
columns 41
cotton 16
Crest of the Wave 49, 92
crochet cotton 14
Cyprus Lace 51, 89

D
Da Puzzle 48, 101
decreasing 20
  purl decreases 21
  three into one 21
  two into one 20
design 32
  charting 36–37
  construction shapes 33–34
  design basics 32

designing a christening
  gown 44
designing a hap shawl 45
designing a scarf 35, 43
designing a stole 35, 42
designing shawls 35
designing with frames 39
designing with one motif in
  multiple ways 40–41
four simple "rules" 33
putting motifs together
  35, 38
swatching 35
what gauge? 32
what patterns? 32
what shape? 32
what size? 32
what yarn? 32
Don's Lace 50, 100
Doris Lace 51, 74
Dot Diamond 49, 82
dressing lace 30
  aftercare 31
  drying and dressing 30
  improvizing 31
  standard laundering
    symbols 31
  storing your lace 31
  washing 30
dressing mats 14
dressing wires 14
Drops Lace 50, 102

E
edges 24
  cast-on edge 26
  charting 36
  garter-stitch edge 26
  knit and tug 24
  slip 1 edge 26
  stockinette-stitch edge 26
  yo, k2togtbl edge 26
ends 19
equipment 14–15
Eyelid Insertion 50, 65

F
Faggotting 48, 53
Fan Lace 51, 116
Fancy Net 49, 50, 51, 56, 72, 74
Feather and Fan 49, 99
Fern 49, 96
Fir Cone 48, 83
Flee Insertion 50, 73
Flee Motif 51, 62
fleece 8–9, 10
frames 39

G
garter stitch
  backgrounds 19
  garter-stitch edge 26
  grafting 25
gauge 16, 32
grafting 25
  Freddy, Teddy 25

garter stitch 25
  practicing in another color 25
  saving yarn 25

H
Hat and Scarf Set 126–128
Hexagon Frame with the
  Brother and the Sister 51, 97
Horse Shoe 48, 76

I
insertions 40
Irish, or Elaine, Lace 50, 113

J
joining yarns 22
  knot and hide 22
  splice and hide 22

K
Kay, Mary 25
Kitchener stitch 25
knitting needles 14, 15
  yarns and needles 16, 17

L
Lace Cable 51, 104
Lace Hole Insertion 50, 66
Lace Holes 50, 51, 54, 103
Ladder 50, 53
Large Diamonds 48, 66
laundering symbols 31
lifelines 19
linen 16

M
Madeira and Diamond 48, 85
Madeira Cascade 49, 114
Margaret's Lace 51, 117
Miniature Leaf 49, 67
mistakes 28
  dropped stitch 28
  extra k2tog—one stitch too
    few 28
  extra yarn over—one stitch
    too many 28
  knit 1 not slip 1 at the start of
    a row 29
  missed yarn over 28
  part of the pattern is
    completely wrong 29
  repairing a break 29
  taking back a large area 29
  taking back a small piece 29
Mitts, Lacy 136–137
mohair 16
motifs 35, 38
  designing with one motif in
    multiple ways 40–41
Mrs Hunter's Pattern 49, 57
Mrs Montague's Pattern 48, 105

N
needle size guides 14, 15
needles 14, 15
New Shell 48, 75

O
Old Shale 48, 108

P
patterns 32
  putting motifs together 35
Peterson, Margaret 117
picking up stitches 26
  attaching a lace to a
    border 27
  cast-on edge 26
  garter-stitch edge 26
  knitting the first row after
    picking up stitches 26
  slip 1 edge 26
  stockinette-stitch edge 26
  yo, k2togtbl edge 26
pins, large-headed 14, 15
Plain Vandyke 50, 88
polyester 16
Print of the Wave 48, 107
projects 120–123
  Baby Set 132–135
  Cobweb Shawl 124–125
  Crescent Shawl 140–141
  Hat and Scarf Set 126–128
  Lacy Mitts 136–137
  Shoulder Shawl 129–131
  Ten-stitch Socks 138–139

Q
Queen's Lace 50, 94

R
Razor Shell 49, 58
Rose Cluster 51, 95
Rose Diamond Frame with
  Rose Clusters 49, 115
Rosebud Eyelid 49, 80
row counters 14

S
scarves 35
  designing a scarf 43
  Hat and Scarf Set 126–128
scissors 14, 15
seams 24
  grafting garter stitch 25
  grafting or Kitchener
    stitch 25
  sewing seams 24
  whip stitch 24
shapes 32
  construction shapes 33–34
  not sure if you have enough
    yarn? 34
shawls 35
  baby shawls 30
  Cobweb Shawl 124–125
  Crescent Shawl 140–141
  designing a hap shawl 45
  Shoulder Shawl 129–131
Shetland lace 8–10
  spinning the wool 10–11
  wedding-ring shawls 10, 11
silk 16

size 32
lip knots 18
Small Diamonds 48, 60
Small Hexagons 49, 68
Small Trees 49, 93
Small Triangle Lace 50, 58
Socks, Ten-stitch 138–139
Spider Insertion 50, 73
Spider Motif 51, 64
Spider's Web 49, 111
spinning 10–11
squares 32
    center out 35
    center square 34
    outside in 35
Steek One 50, 52
Steek Three 50, 52
Steek Two 50, 52
stitch markers 14, 15
    using stitch markers 19
stitches 47
    all-over patterns 48–49
    insertions 50
    lace 50–51
    motifs 51
stockinette-stitch
    backgrounds 19
stoles 35
    designing a stole 42
storing your lace 31
Strawberry 49, 71
swatches 16, 17
    swatch sampler 35

T
techniques 13
    backgrounds 19
    binding off 19
    casting on 18
    changing color 22
    dealing with ends 19
    dealing with mistakes 28–29
    decreases 20–21
    dressing lace 30–31
    edges 24
    joining yarns 22
    lifelines 19
    picking up stitches 26–27
    seams 24–25
    using stitch markers 19
    working from a chart 23
    yarn overs 19
The Madeira 48, 84
The Saltire 51, 118
tools 14–15
Traditional Large Scalloped
    Lace 50, 112
Traditional Peaked Lace 51, 106
Traditional Scalloped Lace
    51, 81
Tree 51, 119
Trellis Diamond 48, 91
triangles 32
    charting 37
    long side down 34
    point up 34

V
Vandyke Lace 50, 61
Vase 51, 98
Victorian Zigzag Lace 51, 103

W
washing lace 30, 31
Wave Lace 50, 87
wedding-ring shawls 10, 11
whip stitch 24
wool 16

Y
yarn overs 19
yarns 11, 16
    blends 17
    joining yarns 22
    not sure if you have enough
        yarn? 34
    pros and cons of different
        fibers 16
    saving yarn 25
    "superwash" fibers 17
    swatches 16, 17
    what yarn? 32
    yarns and needles 16, 17

Z
Zigzag Insertion 50, 69

Abbreviations

fb	front and back
k	knit
knb	knit last st of lace together with next of border
m	make
M	marker
p	purl
PM	place marker
psso	pass slip stitch over
RS	right side (of work)
s	slip
SM	slip marker
st(s)	stitch(es)
tbl	through the back loop(s)
tog	together
WS	wrong side (of work)
yo	yarn over

Symbols

□	k
•	p
V	kfb
O	yo
/	RS: k2tog / WS: ssk
\	RS: ssk / WS: k2tog
⋀	k3togtbl
✳	k last st of lace together with next of border
⊢——⊣	s1, k3, psso
⌢	bind off
□	stitch and row repeat
∀	s1p
⩘	k4togtbl
⫽	k4tog
Ø	drop yo from previous row
∀	slip, then k these sts tog
▩	no st

Credits and resources

For more on Elizabeth Lovick and Shetland lace knitting, visit her website: www.northernlace.co.uk

Many thanks to Jamieson & Smith for generously supplying all the yarn for the stitches in the stitch directory.

These were made using Jamieson & Smith 2-ply lace.

Jamieson
& Smith
100% Shetland Wool
from the Shetland Islands

Many thanks to the following companies for supplying yarn for the projects:

Cobweb Shawl (pages 124–125)
Jamieson & Smith
www.shetlandwoolbrokers.co.uk
1-ply cobweb in Pastel Blue

Hat and Scarf Set (pages 126–128)
Knit Picks
www.knitpicks.com
Reverie in Lavender

Shoulder Shawl (pages 129–131)
Artesano
www.artesanoyarns.co.uk
4-ply alpaca in Anemone, Cream, and Fern

Baby Set (pages 132–135)
Paton's
www.patonsyarns.com
3-ply Fairytale wool in White

Lacy Mitts (pages 137–137)
Lorna's Lace
www.lornaslaces.net
Helen's Lace in Whisper

Ten-stitch Socks (pages 138–139)
Regia
us.schachenmayr.com
Sock Hand-dye effect yarn in 6554
and
Trekking XXL
www.skacelknitting.com
Sock yarn in 415

Crescent Shawl (pages 140–141)
ColourMart
www.colourmart.com
Silk/linen 8/48 in Lime Gold

Recommended needles

Signature Needle Arts
www.signatureneedlearts.com
Stiletto point

addi
www.addinadeln.de
Lace needles

Recommended blocking wires

Handworks
www.handworksnw.com

Heirloom Knitting
www.heirloom-knitting.co.uk

The author would like to thank:

Margaret Peterson from Unst, Shetland, has taught me so much over many years, and also checked the names of the patterns for me. Without her I would know little of the magic of Shetland lace.

I would like to thank the team at Quarto: Kate Kirby, Moira Clinch, Jackie Palmer, Caroline Guest, Julia Shone—and especially my editor, Victoria Lyle. Ashley Knowlton has been the perfect technical editor and any mistakes are mine not hers.

Quarto would like to thank:

The following for supplying images for inclusion in this book:
iStockphotos, p.8b
Shetland Museum Archives, p.9b, 10bl/br
Getty Images, p.11

MOT Models for supplying the model used for the Projects (pages 120–141).

All step-by-step and other images are the copyright of Quarto Publishing plc.

While every effort has been made to credit contributors, Quarto would like to apologize should there have been any omissions or errors—and would be pleased to make the appropriate correction for future editions of the book.